Theory and Research in Teaching

ARNO A. BELLACK, Editor

TEACHERS COLLEGE PRESS
Teachers College, Columbia University
New York, New York

© 1963 BY TEACHERS COLLEGE, COLUMBIA UNIVERSITY

LIBRARY OF CONGRESS CATALOG CARD NUMBER 63-18839

THIRD PRINTING 1970

The two conferences on theory and research in teaching reported in this publication were financed by a grant from the Bailey K. Howard Faculty Research Fund.

PRINTED IN THE UNITED STATES OF AMERICA

FOREWORD

LIKE OTHER FIELDS OF SCHOLARSHIP, EDUCATION HAS EXPERIENCED periodic shifts in the problems that are of central concern to theorists and research workers. One such recent shift in educational research is to be observed in the growing interest in the study of classroom teaching. This interest cannot accurately be called new; it represents rather a renewal of a long-standing concern.

There are, however, certain characteristics of current studies that distinguish them from work undertaken in preceding periods. One prominent feature of contemporary research is emphasis on systematic observation of the classroom activities of students and teachers. In increasing numbers, researchers are focusing attention on the verbal and nonverbal behavior of students and teachers in the classroom, with special attention to the roles, functions, and activities of teachers.

To provide opportunity for discussion of some of the theoretical problems arising out of studies of this kind, the Department of Curriculum and Teaching of Teachers College, Columbia University, sponsored two conferences during 1962, one in the Spring (April 12 and 13) and another in the Fall (November 2 and 3). Researchers engaged in studies of classroom behavior were invited to prepare papers setting forth the conceptual framework within which their studies were planned and carried out. These papers served as the basis for discussion during the conferences and in this report they are now made available to a wider reading audience.

Special thanks go to Mr. Herbert Kliebard, Mr. Ronald Hyman, and Miss Valora Nelson, research assistants at Teachers College, for help in carrying out conference plans. Mr. Kliebard also assisted in editing this volume and preparing the bibliography.

ARNO A. BELLACK

CONTENTS

TOWARD A THEORY OF TEACHING
    by B. Othanel Smith   1

THE EVALUATING OPERATION IN THE CLASSROOM
    by Milton Meux   11

UTAH STUDY OF THE ASSESSMENT OF TEACHING
    by Marie M. Hughes   25

TEACHER INFLUENCE IN THE CLASSROOM
    by Ned A. Flanders   37

THE ANALYSIS OF VERBAL INTERACTION IN THE CLASSROOM
    by Mary Jane McCue Aschner   53

THE SCIENTIFIC STUDY OF TEACHER BEHAVIOR
    by Donald M. Medley and Harold E. Mitzel   79

STUDY OF CHILDREN THROUGH OBSERVATION OF CLASSROOM BEHAVIOR
    by Edna Shapiro   91

ANALYSIS OF TWO KINDERGARTEN SETTINGS
    by Martin Kohn   102

CLASSROOM PROCESSES STUDY
    by Eleanor Leacock   112

BIBLIOGRAPHY   118

TOWARD A THEORY OF TEACHING*

B. OTHANEL SMITH
University of Illinois

WHEN WE BEGAN OUR CURRENT STUDY OF TEACHING, WE HAD ONLY THE vaguest notion of teaching itself and no theory of teaching whatever. Of course, we knew, or at least were familiar with, the theories of teaching found in literature. We were acquainted with Kilpatrick's theory of teaching set forth in his *Foundations of Method* and with Morrison's theory of teaching as elaborated in his *Practice of Teaching in the Secondary School* as well as the more classical theories. We were also familiar with the experimental work to determine the relative effectiveness of methods of teaching. Furthermore, we were quite familiar with the speculations, based on psychological concepts and principles, about how teaching should be carried on. But we had no theory of teaching of our own. And even now after spending over four years in the study of teaching, we are still unable to formulate a theory.

We can do no more than suggest a few concepts which we have found useful in the conduct of our investigations and which might become elements of a teaching theory. They are rather naïve concepts and we shall treat them as such. In doing so, we shall be at a disadvantage. For by speaking at a naïve level, what we say will sound obvious; and if we become sophisticated, what we say will not be clear. The alternatives seem to be a choice between being obvious and being vague and ambiguous. Nevertheless, we shall deal with the ideas which we have found useful, and, at least for the present, say very little about the more complex ideas about which we have thought but of which we have made little use.

* Adopted in part from *A Study of the Logic of Teaching*, by B. O. Smith, et al. Urbana, Ill.: Bureau of Educational Research, College of Education, University of Illinois, 1960.

TEACHING AS DEPENDENT ON PSYCHOLOGY AND PHILOSOPHY

We began with certain biases which took the form of protests against efforts to describe teaching in terms of philosophical and psychological concepts and principles. Let us first set forth these protests and then turn to the more constructive ideas with which we worked.

It is generally assumed that effective ways of teaching can be derived from theories of logic and epistemology. Every theory of teaching described in the literature is based on some conception of either learning or thinking and of the nature of knowledge. For example, Kilpatrick's formulation of method is grounded in Dewey's theory of logic and of knowledge. To be sure, he made extensive use of Thorndike's theory of learning, but this theory is really not an essential part of his account of teaching, as is evidenced by the fact that he later repudiated Thorndike's theory while neither discarding nor modifying his own theory of teaching. Now we do not believe that it is possible to formulate a theory of teaching applicable to the classroom situation by inference from philosophical ideas.

We take the same position with respect to theories of learning. It is often assumed that if we know how learning occurs, we thereby know how to teach. For example, it is generally assumed that if we know how individuals solve problems, then we know how to teach by the problem method. To teach is to see that the individual does the operations that problem solving requires.

Any effort to apply philosophical or scientific knowledge directly to teaching will fail. In order to go from theoretical ideas such as those found in psychology and philosophy to a teaching operation, it is necessary to work out procedures and materials to bridge the gap between the theory and the practice. We cannot go directly from theories to practical applications, because there are particular problems that arise with respect to both materials and procedures. Of course, everyone who attempts to develop teaching by beginning with philosophy and psychology knows this. But what they do not know is that one of the primary conditions for applying any theory is a thorough understanding of the phenomenon to which it is to be applied. It is just as important to understand the phenomenon of teaching as a condition of applying ideas and principles to it from other domains as it is to understand the principles and ideas themselves. We must first identify and describe the various dimensions and variables of teaching behavior before we can think realistically about concepts and principles relevant to its control.

In the next place, we discarded the notion that teaching necessarily entails learning. It is fashionable in educational circles to say that if the student has not learned, the teacher has not taught. And this view is reinforced by speaking of teaching and learning always together as the teaching-learning process. It requires no great amount of reflection to see that a teacher can teach any part of a subject without the student learning what the teacher is trying to teach. Just as one can learn without being taught so can one be taught without learning.

We further discarded the notion that teaching and talking are incompatible. Both pragmatic thought and behavioristic psychology emphasize that learning takes place through activity. This view is popularized in the expression that one learns to do by doing. The import of this view is to deprecate the use of language in teaching. It is fashionable to say that teachers talk too much and that to learn through words rather than experience is mere verbalism. This view is held in spite of the fact that it is difficult, if not impossible, to teach anyone anything without the use of language. And it is equally true that most of the knowledge which we teach in school is expressed in words and other symbolic forms and that apart from the language system, there would be little or no knowledge to teach at all.

Finally it seemed necessary to rid ourselves of the notion that a reality is referred to when the expression "method of teaching" is used. From casual observation of teaching, we came to the conclusion that actual classroom teaching does not conform to the methods of teaching described in textbooks. This conclusion has been sustained by subsequent observation. Actual teaching is so varied, so complex, so fluid as almost to defy any description whatever; and it certainly does not correspond to the concepts of method set forth in treatises on the subject. When we speak of methods of teaching, we are speaking, not about realities, but about the picture of teaching we have built up out of ideas borrowed from psychology and philosophy.

To summarize, we found it necessary to clear the ground of the foregoing notions about the relationship of teaching to learning and to philosophy and psychology, and to eliminate at the same time the ideas that teaching could be carried on without talking and that it could be described by reference to the various methods set forth in books on the subject. This ground clearing opened up the question: What is teaching and how can it be described?

STRATEGY IN TEACHING

A theory of teaching will consist in (*a*) a statement of the variables comprising teaching behavior, (*b*) a formulation of the possible relations among these variables, and (*c*) hypotheses about the relations between the variables comprising teaching behavior and the variables descriptive of the psychological and social conditions within which teaching behavior occurs. Now, the study of teaching which we have been carrying on is designed to identify and describe the variables which make up teaching behavior.

Our most general notion is that teaching is everywhere the same, that it is a natural social phenomenon and is fundamentally the same from one culture to another and from one time to another in the same culture. In our view, teaching is a system of action involving an agent, a situation, an end-in-view, and two sets of factors in the situation—one set over which the agent has no control (for example, size of classroom and physical characteristics of pupils) and one set which the agent can modify with respect to the end-in-view (for example, assignments and ways of asking questions).

The set of factors which the agent can control constitutes the means by which the end-in-view is reached. The means, in turn, consists in two types of factors: (*a*) subject matter and instructional paraphernalia, and (*b*) the ways of manipulating and maneuvering the types of factors in *a*. The first of these we call material means and the second procedural means. Our investigation of teaching is concerned with procedural means alone.

The procedural means have two aspects: large-scale maneuvers which we call strategies, and smaller movements—constituting tactical elements of strategies—which we call logical operations.

The term "strategy" refers to a pattern of acts that serves to attain certain outcomes and to guard against certain others. Among the general objectives toward which a strategy may be directed are the following: to ensure that certain learnings will be acquired in as brief a time as possible; to induce students to engage in exchange of ideas; and to minimize the number of wrong responses as the student attempts to learn a concept, principle, etc. Of course, a strategy may be used, and in fact usually is used, to ensure the attainment of certain content objectives, for example, to learn what policy Andrew Jackson might follow with respect to federal aid to highways were he now president.

We are just beginning our study of strategies, and the concept of a strategy is only in the formative stage. While we cannot give a definition of the term "strategy" at the moment, we can perhaps clarify the use of the term to some extent. There are times when a teacher desires his students to engage in an exchange of ideas. On such an occasion, he is not concerned, or at least he is not primarily concerned, that they acquire a particular substantive learning. Rather, he wishes the students to engage in discussion and to learn to listen and to challenge each other's ideas. Now one of the ways of engaging the students in such discussion is to raise contrary-to-fact questions and issues. Suppose the teacher asks what position might Andrew Jackson take with respect to federal aid to highways were he now president. This question is relatively open, because of the fact that no correct answer can really be given to the question. But the students will be able to make various conjectures as to what position Jackson would now take, based on knowledge of what he did do when he was president and of his general temperament and character. The general strategy in this case is to raise a question for which there is no clearcut answer and for which there cannot be such an answer, and then to follow it up with maneuvers designed to maintain discussion rather than to drive home answers.

To take another example, the teacher may begin with open-ended questions such as: What are some possible explanations of the Civil War? The strategy here is to put the question in such a way as to focus the attention of the students on possible causes rather than on what the teacher has in mind as the causes. Had the teacher asked the question in this way—What were the causes of the Civil War? Or, what caused the Civil War?—the attention of the student would be directed either to what the book says, or to what the teacher has in mind and which the students are supposed to match in their answers. When questions are open-ended, students are more apt to express their own ideas rather than engage in a guessing game with the teacher.

The concept of strategy in teaching can be clarified by studying teaching behavior, and, from such a study, determining the criteria to be used in identifying actual strategies as they appear in the classroom. While we approach our study of the strategies of teaching with some rough notion of what we mean by the term, these notions will be refined and sharpened as we observe teaching behavior. In this way we hope to build a set of criteria which will have a fair degree of reliability. Once we are able to identify strategies objectively by means of the criteria, then it will be possible by analyzing these strategies to determine their structure and dynamics. We believe that once strategies have been described in this way, it will then be possible to use the concept of strategy in experimental work.

TACTICAL ASPECTS OF TEACHING

The smaller movements constituting the tactical elements of strategies we call episodes. Episodes are pedagogically significant units of classroom discourse. They are made up of two or more utterances, an utterance being defined as what any one individual says at a given time. The simplest form of an episode consists of an opening which we call an entry, and an end which we call a close. Between the entry and the close is one utterance, usually by a student. Here is an illustration of the simplest form of an episode.

TEACHER: When was Sir Isaac Newton born?
STUDENT: 1642.
TEACHER: Okeh.

The first utterance of the teacher is the entry, and the second teacher's utterance is the close. The student's utterance makes up the body of the episode. In more complicated forms, the body of the episode consists of more than one utterance, and, of course, the more utterances in the body of the episode, the more complex it is.

Episodes are verbal exchanges between two or more persons. These exchanges take two different forms, giving rise to two types of episodes. In the first type, the exchange is between two persons who are alternately responding to each other. The teacher, let us say, asks a question. The student responds. The teacher then responds to what the student says, and the student in turn reacts to the teacher's remarks, the exchange finally terminating in a closing remark, usually by the teacher. This sort of exchange comprises what we call reciprocating episodes. In the second type, the verbal exchange involves more than two speakers. They respond to the entry rather than to each other, and the responses are thus coordinated with one another. We call this sort of unit a coordinating episode. The coordinating form exhibits greater student initiative and flexibility than does the reciprocating episode.

In addition to episodes, there is a unit of discourse which we call a monologue. It is an utterance made by either the teacher or the student, and stands alone. It is a solo performance requiring no entry to kick it off, and calling for no response. The most complete form of monologue would, of course, be an extended lecture. Our data show that there are comparatively few monologues and very little lecturing in high school classrooms.

Episodes may be viewed either from a logical or a psychological standpoint. Psychologically, an episode represents a gap to be filled with information. The entry of the episode consists in giving a bit of information—usually a subject and an end or outcome, more or less implicit in the entry. The filling of the gap between the entry and the closing constitutes the behavior which the episode calls for.

Episodes may be either completely closed or completely open. And there are episodes with varying degrees of openness falling between these two extremes. In a closed episode, the gap can be filled with only one bit of information. There are no alternative ways of filling the gap. For example, in a biology class the teacher asks: What are the pons? What does the word "pons" mean? A pupil answers: Bridges. The teacher then says: It means bridge or a connecting link. Now in this episode there is very little choice of response. The student could have said "connecting link" instead of "bridges," or he might have been able to find some other synonomous expression. But even so this episode is relatively closed for the student has very little choice among ways of filling the gap.

An open episode encourages a great variety of responses. Suppose a teacher were to ask a ninth-grade science class: Can you devise a way to hear a fly walk? Now this entry contains very little information, save an end-in-view. But it does require a great variety of information in order to attain the end. A situation such as this is almost completely open. The students must read, observe, and think a great deal about ways of magnifying the noise made by a fly when it walks. Here is another example. In one of our episodes, a pupil asks: What do we mean by thinking? The teacher replies: Maybe planning something, or thinking about something, or recalling past things. A pupil then says: Thinking about something. And another pupil says: Just having a thought. Now this episode is relatively open because the vagueness of the term "thinking"—together with the great variety of uses of the term—make it possible to fill the gap between the entry and the close in a large number of ways. Had the students been more sophisticated with respect to the concept of thinking, quite a long discussion might have ensued and thinking might have been viewed from a large number of standpoints. The vagueness and ambiguity of the term could have been explored at considerable length. It is possible to cite a number of other examples showing varying degrees of openness.

It is not difficult to see that episodes of the closed type lend themselves very easily to programmed instruction such as that used in so-called teaching machines where the situations are so structured as to reduce the chance of incorrect responses. In sharp contrast, episodes of the more open forms lend themselves to manipulation by those teachers who wish to encourage originality and flexibility in their students. It seems reasonable to suppose that openness of episodes tends, in the various sciences, to encourage creativity and, in those fields which deal with social concerns, to stimulate the growth of wisdom.

TACTICAL ELEMENTS AS LOGICAL OPERATIONS

Episodes may also be viewed as logical operations. In other words, episodes are classifiable in terms of their similarity to ideal logical operations whose performance is governed by rules.

Logical operations are a form of rule-guided behavior. This is a form of behavior, correctible by criteria, in which definite limits are set and the chances of behaving ineffectively are reduced. Such behavior may be distinguished from other forms of behavior, such as forgetting one's car keys, striking out in anger, running from a fright situation, and all sorts of mannerisms. Each of these behaviors results from some set of conditions and is in no way guided by rules. On the other hand, when we drive on the right side of the road, or when we move the pawn forward one square in chess, or when we use a singular verb with a singular subject, we are engaging in rule-guided behavior. It is possible to say of such behavior that it is either correct or incorrect. On the other hand, non-rule-guided behavior, such as forgetting one's car keys, cannot be said to be either correct or incorrect. It just is, or it is not.

Now, as we have suggested, logical operations are capable of correction by rules. If the teacher is aware of logical operations and knows the rules by which they are performed, he will be able to monitor his behavior insofar as these operations are involved in it. He will be able to think about his behavior together with that of students and to assess and correct these behaviors by reference to the rules of their governance.

We have made a rather extensive study of teaching behavior with the view to identifying the logical operations involved in it, and we are now attempting to describe these operations from a theoretical standpoint. We have been able to identify twelve logical operations, as follows: Defining, describing, designating, stating, reporting, comparing and contrasting, substituting, classifying, opining, valuing, conditional inferring, and explaining.

Logical operations are often very simple. For example, consider the following operation of defining. What does the word "principle" mean? The student says: A rule. Then the teacher says: Yes, a rule, a theory, an idea. Now this is a relatively simple operation involving the mere substitution of one word for another. In such case, no new concept is introduced and all that is involved is the mere use of synonyms.

But a logical operation can be very complex. For example, the operation of defining can become very involved when it is used to develop a concept. We sometimes forget that the development of a definition is one of the ways by which concepts are developed as well as related. Let us suppose that the question of the meaning of the term "imperialism" arises in class. Most high school students already possess some sort of meaning for this term. But the concept would need to be refined and its symbolic expression made more rigorous. This can be done in class by engaging students in the process of working out criteria by which to decide whether or not a given country is to be classified as an imperialistic nation. The teacher may proceed by listing a number of nations and then raising the question as to which, if any, belong in the category of imperialistic countries. As the students decide that one nation or another belongs either in or out of the category, the teacher asks for the criteria by which the decisions are being made. These criteria may then be written on the board. As the students consider country after country, the list of criteria will be built up, refined, and made more rigorous in expression. As all of this is done, the concept of imperialism itself becomes clearer, and more useful to the students.

Now, there are certain rules of defining which would be of use to the teacher as he proceeds with the instructional process. Some of these rules are formal, that is to say, they are the rules by which the term "definition" itself is understood. For example, a formal rule would be that a definition is a rule for the use of a term. Then there are epistemic rules to be used in monitoring and governing the process of defining. These rules tell whether or not a given definition is to be accepted or not. If the definition meets these rules, we can say that from a logical standpoint it is correct. For example, one epistemic rule would be the following: A classificatory definition must not be circular, that is to say, it must not include in the defining part of the definition, the term which is to be defined. In addition to formal and epistemic rules, there are pragmatic rules for defining. A pragmatic rule has to do with the relation of the definition to the purpose or audience for which the definition is intended. For example, a pragmatic rule is as follows: The definition should be expressed in terms understandable by the individuals for whom it is intended. All the logical operations we have studied are governed by these three different kinds of rules. And it seems reasonable to claim that the teacher is better able to handle these operations and to monitor the behavior of both himself and his students in the performance of these operations, if he is familiar with these rules.

There is another dimension of logical operations as they occur in teaching. It is that the operations may be performed in several different ways. There are five or six different ways of explaining, and there are several ways of defining. For example, there are teleological explanations, causal explanations, normative explanations, sequent explanations, procedural explanations, and mechanical explanations. These various forms of explaining have their own peculiarities, and while they are subject to certain rules in common, they are nevertheless governed in some respects by different rules. The same observation can be made with respect not only to defining, but to the other logical operations we have studied.

In closing, it should be pointed out that the description of teaching set forth above is not to be understood as a comprehensive view. Teaching behavior is extremely varied, and the concepts suggested in the foregoing discussion cover only a narrow band of such behavior. It includes only a part of the cognitive aspects of teaching.

Our description does not include affective elements such as modes of ingratiation and of reinforcement, nor does it deal with nonverbal forms of teaching behavior. Neither do the concepts set forth describe teaching as a process of showing as in such cases as showing students how to type, how to hold a tennis racket, or how to do a sum in arithmetic. Teachers also use all sorts of physical equipment to illustrate scientific principles, or to engage students in the task of thinking through scientific problems, but this aspect of teaching is left out of our account. Nevertheless, it is believed that the concepts suggested above will enable us to deal with most of the behavior manifested in the teaching of the so-called content subjects—mathematics, social studies, English, and science.

We are a long way from a comprehensive theory of teaching grounded in a clear-cut system of concepts and backed up by empirical evidence. To develop a general theory, if indeed it is possible at all, will require bold explorations which take account of what has been done, but which are in no way bound by past failures and successes.

THE EVALUATING OPERATION IN THE CLASSROOM

MILTON MEUX
University of Illinois

THIS PAPER PRESENTS AN ANALYSIS[1] OF THE LOGICAL OPERATION OF evaluating as it occurs in the classroom. Evaluating is one of twelve logical operations identified and described in a recent project concerned with a logical analysis of teaching. This project was described in its general outlines at this conference last year. It will be recalled that the basis of classification for these twelve logical operations was the kind of ideal response required by the entry of the episode. In this paper, however, the focus shifts to an analysis and classification of the actual responses in the continuing phase of the episode.

Evaluation permeates much of our everyday lives. In fact, practically anything can be and is evaluated at some time or another, in some context. This pervasiveness is reflected in the classroom. Although only about 5 per cent of the episodes we have studied are classified in the Evaluating category, the variety of things evaluated and the terms in which they are evaluated are quite marked, as may be seen in the Criteria for Evaluating Entries, appended to this paper.

THE LOGICAL NATURE OF EVALUATING

Because of the variety of things evaluated, contexts, and evaluative terms, it is impossible to give a satisfactory general definition of evaluating

[1] The analysis reported here was made pursuant to a contract with the U.S. Office of Education, and carried on under the direction of Professor B. Othanel Smith through the Bureau of Educational Research of the College of Education, University of Illinois. The author wishes to acknowledge the assistance of B. Othanel Smith and Jerrold R. Coombs in clarifying many of the points in this analysis.

which will serve to identify an evaluating episode. Briefly, it is one in which the student or teacher appraises or rates something, or one in which a value matter is raised in some way, such as to ask whether there is agreement on an issue, answer, etc.

Although many technical distinctions have been made among the various aspects of evaluating, our episodic material justifies distinguishing only four logical elements of evaluating: (1) something such as an object, statement, expression, event, action, or state of affairs—designated hereafter as T_e for convenience—to be evaluated; (2) an evaluation of T_e in terms such as good, unjust, false, desirable, etc.; (3) a warrant by which the evaluation is supported, backed, or justified; and (4) facts, called connecting facts, about T_e which show the connection of T_e to the warrant and thereby support its use in evaluating T_e.

These four elements may be represented in diagrammatic form as follows:[2]

MODEL OF EVALUATING

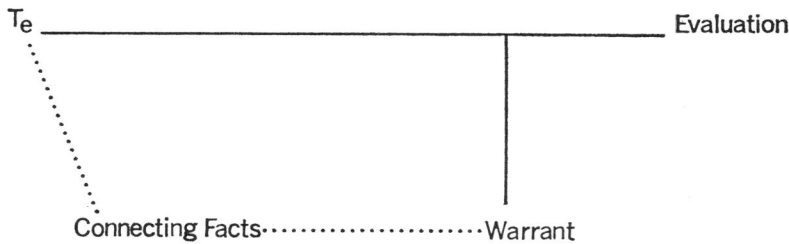

PROBLEMS OF ANALYSIS

The precise character of the logical elements of evaluating and the relations of one element to another depend so greatly on the context in which the evaluation is made that we could not hope to present here an exhaustive or even exclusive classification of the various kinds of evaluating. Rather, we shall present what seem to us to be typical patterns or kinds of evaluation that occur in the classroom, using rather broad and necessarily vague divisions. As with the development of our other logical categories, only episodes on our tapes have been used as the basis for this classification scheme.

Since the analysis in this paper is to focus on actual responses in the continuing phase of the episode, our classification must be based on dis-

[2] Suggested by Stephen Toulmin's *The Use of Argument* (Cambridge, England: Cambridge University Press, 1958).

tinctions of some kind in at least one of the four logical elements discussed above.[3] Briefly the rationale for our choice is as follows:

Evaluating episodes vary in the amount of material they contain on each of the four logical elements of evaluating: T_e, the evaluation, the warrant, and the connecting facts. All the episodes contain at least two elements, T_e and the evaluation; many contain only these two elements. In view of this situation, it is tempting to propose these two elements as the basis of classification. Yet it is doubtful that distinctions made in either of these elements could be a sound basis for a logically significant classification scheme. The same is true of connecting facts, since they cannot be stated meaningfully except in the context of a warrant. This leaves distinctions among warrants as the remaining consideration.

Very few episodes contain warrants as such. However, in many episodes facts are stated which are apparently intended to serve as warrants. At first blush the comments in the episode seem more like defending, clarifying, elaborating, or just commenting on the evaluation given. Further analysis, however, discloses that these comments are used as, or function as, warrants. In many contexts, the statement of connecting facts is clearly meant to imply a warrant suitable for the context. In spite of these difficulties, we have chosen the kind of warrant as the most significant basis for our classification scheme. The warrant, as grounds or backing for the evaluation, is the one logical element most relevant to assessing the correctness of the evaluation, and it is the correctness of responses which has been the main concern in our project.

KINDS OF EVALUATING

The four kinds of evaluating we have analyzed, based on the kinds of warrants, will now be presented, with episodes illustrating each kind.

APPLICATION OF RULES

In this kind of evaluating something is evaluated in terms of whether it conforms to a rule. This rule, then, is the warrant. The rule may be a deductive or mathematical rule, a rule of evidence, a grammatical rule,

---

[3] Not only are many areas and matters of evaluation raised in the classroom, but the ways they are introduced in the entries also vary greatly. Some entries ask directly for evaluations, other entries are less direct: they may ask whether another student agrees, whether something is really or actually the case, etc. Some entries ask for an evaluation, others ask the student merely to affirm or deny a given evaluation. It is possible that this variation in the form of the entry has some logical or pedagogical significance. If so, how much? Does it justify inclusion in the initial efforts toward a classification scheme? Whatever the significance of the variation in entries, we have chosen to ignore these variations in our present analysis.

etc. Evaluating the validity of an argument, the correctness of a mathematical proof, the correctness of sentence structure, and the truth of a statement or set of statements all involve the application of some kind of rule.

There were three sorts of rules in evaluating episodes which involved the application of rules to support the evaluation: formal rules, grammatical rules, and evidential rules (rules of evidence).

Formal rules. This kind of evaluating involves both logical and mathematical rules. Logical rules include the rules of deduction, the so-called laws of logic (excluded middle, noncontradiction, identity), substitution, etc. Mathematical rules include rules of addition, subtraction, various geometrical theorems, etc. Application of formal rules is exemplified in evaluating an argument as valid by applying the well-known rules of deduction, checking each point of the argument where a deduction is involved.

The few episodes of this kind that involve logical rules are quite elliptical—omitting explicit statements of both connecting facts and warrants—and even involve erroneous evaluation of arguments and application of supposedly well-known logical matters. Surprisingly enough, there were no evaluating episodes which used or referred to mathematical rules.[4] (However, there were many episodes from other categories—such as Stating, Describing, and Explaining—which employed mathematical rules in some way.)

The following episode illustrates the use of a logical rule.[5] The teacher in a sociology class has just reported a statement by J. Edgar Hoover to the effect that the crime problem is a youth problem.

EPISODE 1

TEACHER: [Does] that agree with what you think, Sue?

SUE: I read, let's see in the paper, I think it was a month or two ago where he just contradicted himself because he said that the teen-agers weren't all at fault. I mean that they weren't committing the most crimes, and that some bad kids were just shoving around the good kids and that they were all getting blamed by the teen-agers weren't as bad as they thought they were. So he wrote that and he wrote this too. He's just contradicting himself. So he must not know.

LIZ: . . . teen-agers, that doesn't mean much.

---

[4] This may be accounted for partly by this particular teacher's habit or strategy of not asking directly for an evaluation—e.g., "What is the correct answer to the third problem?"—but rather asking the student to repeat an operation—e.g., "What is that answer again?"—so that he sees the mistake himself; the teacher also asks the students just for answers instead of for right or correct answers, etc.

[5] In the episodes presented in this paper, partially inaudible phrases and passages too garbled to transcribe are indicated by brackets and dots, respectively.

TEACHER: In one of the other reports given in 5th period, J. Edgar Hoover was quoted again and he stated that 97% of the teen-agers were good law-abiding citizens, which may be on your side, Sue. And I think speaks well for the great majority of teen-agers. But it's this other 3% or so that brings the bad name upon the group.

In this episode Sue points out a contradiction in two statements apparently made by Hoover, one that teen-agers commit the most crimes and the other that they don't. The rule involved here—not explicitly—is the so-called "law of noncontradiction."

Grammatical rules. This kind of evaluating involves grammatical rules, which specify subject-verb agreement, which parts of speech modify others, sentence structure, etc. For example, the adverb "quickly" is used correctly to modify the verb "run" in the sentence "The fox runs quickly."

These episodes are easy to identify, as seen in the following example from an English class discussing how one part of speech modifies another.

EPISODE 2

TEACHER: Anyone want to disagree? Bill.
BILL: "Good" adds to "employment."
TEACHER: Well, that's true.

In this episode "good" is shown by the teacher to be an adjective modifying the noun "employment." As with all episodes of this sort the rule—adjectives modify nouns—is not stated explicitly, but is fairly clear from the context.

Evidential rules. In this kind of evaluating are inductive rules and rules of evidence for establishing the truth of propositions, hypotheses, statements, etc. These evidential rules include Mills's methods, modern statistical methods, and various aspects of scientific method in general. Evidential rules, of course, are not formal in character as are logical and mathematical rules.

The following episode illustrates this kind of evaluation.

EPISODE 3

TEACHER: Any one of you have any questions you'd like to ask? Betty? . . . Brian?
BRIAN: This sort of—the author's mentioned. . . . Betty brought out that newspapers always tell the truth. I'm not arguing with you—I'm arguing with the author there. With the author of the article, because newspapers don't always tell the truth.
BETTY: Well, he says—you know—you look in the newspaper. . . . [back after] years.
BRIAN: I mean, over all, yes, but I don't think that all newspapers tell the truth.

BETTY: It says that you—you should look into it as a duty. I mean be alive to conditions as—they to conditions as they do exist. You know, if you look at the newspaper you know something about it, not that it tells you the truth.

BRIAN: It's common for the newspaper to use propaganda to just give one side of the picture. I mean there—there wouldn't be libel suits if they always told the truth.

In this episode the warrant seems to be that suggested in Brian's last utterance, that truth is obtained or approximated when more than one side of the picture is presented: ". . . it's common for the newspaper to use propaganda, to just give one side of the picture."

COMPARISON WITH CRITERIA

In this kind of evaluation T_e is compared with or is assessed in terms of a criterion or set of criteria.[6] The warrant, then, is the criterion or set of criteria. For example, a good apple has certain criteria such as redness, firmness, a certain range of flavor, etc.; a good automobile has certain criteria such as speed of acceleration, a certain degree of braking power, bright headlights, etc.

The following episodes illustrate this kind of evaluation.

EPISODE 4

TEACHER: Were they able to adequately outfit these men for—service? Suppose they'd had—oh let's say 50,000 men that volunteered. Would they have been able to get them ready for service down here in Cuba? Now, the Navy was well-organized and could take care of things. Was the army well-organized? Dick?

DICK: No.

TEACHER: No, the quartermaster's—department was very much behind the . . . in their procedures and in their ability to take care of these people. Actually, they didn't have very many summer uniforms, and one of the problems that these men—these volunteers who went to Florida—you see, this was coming into spring and into summer, and here they were with winter uniforms and down in semi-tropical territory where it was extremely warm, and the wool uniforms weren't very comfortable. They did not have adequate . . . much ammunition and—uh—while that part of it was more easily remedied than some of the other things, they were—uh—certainly not too adequately outfitted—uh—in the—uh—beginning of the war and could not have stood a tremendous increase of—uh—men.

[6] For a detailed discussion of this kind of evaluating, considered more broadly, see J. O. Urmson, "On grading," in Antony Flew, *Logic and Language* (2nd Series; Oxford, England: Basil Blackwell, 1959).

Evaluating Operation in the Classroom

EPISODE 5

TEACHER: Jake?

JAKE: It doesn't seem to me that the way John Quincy Adams became president wasn't—sort of what I would feel a fair way.

TEACHER: Well, I was going to ask that of Rick. What is your judgment of . . . in '24?

RICK: Oh, that—the—requirement. Well, this country is built so that any man can back anyone he pleases, and it's his privilege to do that, and if he can't do it—well—he should be able to—even though it doesn't seem right. I mean what're we talking about now? . . . Adams as president, had power to pick his cabinet, and he should have done it.

In Episode 4 the army is evaluated in terms of implied criteria of a well-organized army—especially the efficiency of the quartermaster's department in supplying uniforms appropriate to the season, in providing adequate ammunition, and providing for a sudden and "tremendous" increase in the size of the army. In Episode 5 the way in which Adams became President is defended as fair by two criteria: our American tradition that any man can back anyone he pleases, and the President can pick his cabinet as he sees fit. However, the student gives no connecting facts showing how the criteria fit this situation.

APPEAL TO PERSONAL FACTORS

In this kind of evaluation there is no appeal to objective (suprapersonal) warrants such as rules, norms, standards, criteria, etc. Rather, the evaluation is supported or defended only in terms of a warrant such as personal feelings, likings, desires, preferences, etc. For example, a person considers cauliflower a good food just because he likes it.

Two examples of this kind of evaluation are as follows:

EPISODE 6

TEACHER: And this would be desirable? Black supremacy?

BOY: To him [John Kumalo] it would. I mean, that's what he wants—I mean that's what the black people would want, but . . . .

EPISODE 7

TEACHER: Do you approve of that?

ALAN: Oh, I don't know. I like to fight and wrestle . . . and stuff like that. I mean it's all right if they don't really get hurt—uh—hurt each other real bad.

In Episode 6 the "support" of the desirability of black supremacy is "what the black people would want." In Episode 7 a mother encouraging her son to fight back is approved—in the first part of the utterance—on the basis of Alan's own liking of fighting and wrestling.

EXAMINATION OF CONSEQUENCES

In its simplest form there are two distinct aspects to this kind of evaluation: The first aspect is the determination of the consequences or outcome of T_e, where T_e is usually an act, event, process, practice, custom, etc. The second aspect is evaluating the consequences or outcome of T_e in terms of one of the other kinds of evaluation—application of rules, comparison with criteria, or appeal to personal factors.[7] This second aspect constitutes the warrant. For example, spanking may be considered undesirable because the long-term effects of resentment toward authorities leads to unsocial behavior.

Although the consequences of T_e may in one sense be considered as connecting facts, thus seemingly reducing Examination of Consequences to one of the three kinds of evaluation already presented, there is a difference which we consider important enough to maintain this as a distinct kind of evaluation. Here the characteristics or features of T_e itself are not considered and compared with criteria, as in "comparison with criteria." Rather, it is the conditions or state of affairs brought about by T_e that are considered.

This kind of evaluation is often found in more complex form than that described above. For one thing, the outcome of T_e may have already occurred or it might have been predicted. Second, either the intended effect or the actual outcome of T_e may be considered. Finally, T_e itself may be considered only as a means—and thus not evaluated directly—or T_e itself might be evaluated directly. In these more complex cases, one must take account of and balance all the factors in the situation to arrive at a sound evaluation of T_e.

The following episodes are concerned with examining consequences.

EPISODE 8

TEACHER: Now, do you think that this is effective writing? What does he achieve by doing this? Nancy?

NANCY: Well, I think it makes you think when you are just reading through it and not . . . and that this way you have to think whether he is telling the truth or being ironical.

TEACHER: You do respond to this, then? It does provoke something in you?

NANCY: Yes.

TEACHER: All right.

---

[7] For a discussion of this kind of evaluating, see John Dewey, *Theory of Valuation* (Chicago: University of Chicago Press) and *International Encyclopedia of Unified Service,* Vol. II, No. 4.

Evaluating Operation in the Classroom 19

EPISODE 9
TEACHER: Is it fair for an author to use emotional appeal, in which to promote his argument?
LYDIA: I think it definitely is, because if things . . . appeal, and if you can't get people interested in emotion, then you can't promote a cause. Once you get people interested, then you can appeal to their reason also.
TEACHER: You have to get their attention first by appealing to their emotions?
GIRL: I think you do.

In Episode 8 the writing is called effective because it results in provoking thought, it "makes you think." In Episode 9 the use of emotional appeal in an argument is judged to be fair on the basis of its consequences—getting people interested in order then to appeal to their reason.

DEFICIENCIES IN OCCURRENCE AND HANDLING OF EVALUATING IN THE CLASSROOM

The following discussion of logical elements is to be understood only as logical criticism, not an evaluation of the teaching from a pedagogical standpoint. Whether or not teaching behavior would have a more desirable effect if it conformed more closely to logical models is an empirical question beyond the scope of this paper and even of this project. The main concern here is with a logical analysis of evaluating as it occurs in the classroom.

NO WARRANT GIVEN

In many episodes no warrant at all is given for the evaluation. In a few cases, however, the warrant is not given in the evaluating episode itself, but in a later episode, usually in response to an entry such as "Well, why do you think that is a just law?," which would be classified in Explaining.

In the following episodes, no warrant is given for the evaluation.

EPISODE 10
TEACHER: You were mentioning that there was nothing in there to indicate what part was committed by adults. Were those figures that you give us, those that show the percentages committed by—percentages of crimes committed by teen-agers?
LIZ: Yes.

EPISODE 11
TEACHER: If they say that higher wages will cause the mines to close down, now, what argument could he use? Higher wages would cause the mines to close down, therefore, that is why we're not getting higher wages. Isn't that what the cause is? Now what argument could he use—against

the people who were saying that if they have to raise the wages, they'll have to close the mines down? Is it good argument to say "our poverty is what is keeping the mines going"? Isn't there a better, more logical argument against saying the mines will close down if the wages are higher?

JUDY: You could turn it around, and say that—

TEACHER: Well, you're on the right track. Not quite, but keep going.

JUDY: Well, if they don't want a percentage, they want it all. And if they can't get it all, then they—then they'll close down the mines. Because they don't want just a share of it.

In Episode 10 the lack of any warrant seems unimportant, since it is fairly obvious. In Episode 11, however, no warrant is given for "a better, more logical argument." Since whatever warrant the teacher may have had in mind is not clear from what is said or from the context, the student may be confused, especially since the teacher is using the terms in an unusual sense.

FACTUAL STATEMENTS WITH NO WARRANT

In some episodes, a statement of the connecting facts is given, and no warrant is offered to support the evaluation. In some cases this is fairly satisfactory, since in the particular context the statement of the facts by implication almost provides a warrant. Such was the case with Episode 4—with the entry, "Was the army well-organized?"—given above as an example of "Comparison with Criteria."

In other episodes, however, the omission of a warrant and the statement of irrelevant facts is clearly inadequate to support the warrant, and confuses the whole evaluating issue. An example of such an episode is as follows:

EPISODE 12

TEACHER: A big jail. This is *why* the law here is ready, isn't it? And the law is firm and the law is *law,* so to speak. Is it true?

GIRL: No.

TEACHER: No! Things are very lax around here, but the big jail is something that makes the people feel better. All right.

INAPPROPRIATE WARRANT

The teacher or students practically never question or examine critically the warrant given for an evaluation. This may be true even if the criteria are not even the appropriate criteria for an evaluative term used. This may be seen clearly in Episode 9—entry: "Is it fair for an author to use emotional appeal, in which to promote his argument?" In this

Evaluating Operation in the Classroom

episode the kind of warrant appealed to involves just consequences, whereas ordinarily the criteria for "fair" include much more than this, such as various traditions, taking advantage of weaknesses of people, etc.

Inappropriate criteria, not challenged or in any way questioned by the teacher, may be seen also in the following episode, which illustrates poor handling of criteria for a moral judgment. Moral judgments are not usually made on the basis of such personal qualities as unlikable, emotional, and being a ham.

EPISODE 13

TEACHER: This is weakness, isn't it?
BOY: No.
TEACHER: Would you say he was a bad man?
BOY: Yes.
TEACHER: He's not admirable, that's for sure.
BOY: He's not completely unlikable.
TEACHER: He's not completely unlikable.
BOY: He's pretty emotional.
SECOND BOY: He's a ham.
TEACHER: I think that's fair to say. All right.

RELIANCE ON PERSONAL FACTORS

In some episodes evaluative terms are used which require nonpersonal criteria to support the evaluation. If personal factors are relied on exclusively in such cases, the evaluation clearly is not supported adequately. For example, in Episode 6—entry: "And this would be desirable? Black supremacy?"—the reliance on personal factors seems clearly inadequate, since at least the possible consequences and conflict with strong traditions should be considered. On the other hand, in the following episode the use of personal factors seems more suitable.

EPISODE 14

TEACHER: Anyone have any question that you'd like to ask Liz about the article she quoted from? Were there any things in there that seemed to you to be rather shocking as far as statistics is concerned that she gave? Were they as you had expected them to be?
LIZ: Well, that 1,000 cars a week, that really shocked me when I discovered that. Can hardly believe that.

DISCUSSION

Here we would like to discuss briefly some matters having to do with the kinds of evaluating we have presented.

MORAL AND ESTHETIC EVALUATION

The reader, after examining our kinds of evaluating, is likely to wonder what happened to moral evaluation and esthetic evaluation. This requires some comment.

We only have about five episodes which seem to involve moral evaluation, three of which contain no criteria or facts at all, one which does but is very unclear, and one which merely states facts which could be interpreted as reasons or criteria. We have only two episodes which seem to involve esthetic evaluation, neither of which contained any criteria. Since we have so little basis for examining the kinds of evaluation involved in these episodes, we have not considered it sound or fruitful to develop other classes for these episodes. Furthermore, little seems to be lost if each of these episodes is placed in one of our present classes. Thus, in view of these considerations, we have not proposed a separate class for moral or esthetic evaluations. In future work and on the basis of further evidence, however, we may wish to modify this position accordingly.

RULES FOR THE KINDS OF EVALUATING

The four kinds of evaluating differ significantly with respect to how their correctness or soundness is assessed.

Application of rules. Here the rules themselves provide the basis for determining correctness, the rules which support the evaluation—e.g., the various deductive rules, mathematical theorems, grammatical rules which form the basis of the category itself.

Comparison with criteria. We have been unable as yet to clarify the ways for determining correctness in this kind of evaluating. There are, of course, ways of checking or validating these evaluations, such as agreement among experts. Furthermore, if the criteria can be specified in completely nonevaluative terms, then whether T_e satisfies the criteria is essentially decided according to evidential rules.

Appeal to personal factors. There apparently seem to be no ways for determining the correctness of these evaluations, since they are psychological reactions, dispositions, feeling, etc.

Examination of consequences. The first aspect of this kind of evaluating, determining the consequences of T_e, is a "factual" or "predictive" matter; here evidential rules are the relevant ones. The second aspect, evaluating the consequences of T_e, involves or reduces to one or more of the other three kinds of evaluating.

It is interesting to note that the first three kinds of evaluating can be arranged on a continuum of the degree of subjectivity or personal factors involved in the kind of warrant. At one end of the continuum, there is little or no subjectivity: the warrant is "completely logical." For example, the validity of an argument depends only on the logical relations among the premises and the conclusion, and not on the feelings or preferences of any person. At the other end of the continuum, there is a great deal of subjectivity: the warrant consists of personal preferences, likings, cathexes, etc., with no logical rules or objective standards involved. For example, a person thinks boxing is a good sport because he enjoys it.

CONFLICTS AMONG KINDS OF EVALUATION

Since a thing may be evaluated by any one of the four kinds of evaluating, there are many situations where at least two of the kinds of evaluating are used by different parties, leading to confusion or dispute.

We know of no general rules or criteria by which it can be decided which is the correct kind of evaluating in any particular situation.

APPENDIX
CRITERIA FOR EVALUATING ENTRIES

Perhaps the most reliable (but not completely dependable) verbal cue to these entries is the occurrence of such words as "bad," "good," "mistake," "right," "safe," "true," "freedom," "strong," "new."

CRITERIA AND EXAMPLES

A. The entry asks whether the action (decision, feeling, etc.) of an individual or group is right, just, democratic, strong, etc.
   1. Do you think President Truman did right when he removed General MacArthur?
   2. Was the sit-down strike a sensible thing?
B. The entry asks whether an institution, law, social policy, or practice is right, just, good, bad, etc.
   1. Is a law requiring a person to belong to a union bad?
   2. Didn't the anti-trust legislation rob people of their rights?
   3. Do you think the parliamentary system is very good in emergencies?
C. The entry asks whether a physical or biological object or characteristic is important, valuable, etc.
   1. Is the fact that man has the thumb very important?
   2. Do you think that silicon is very valuable to American industries?

D. The entry asks whether an operation is satisfactory, a bit of evidence is sufficient or adequate, or an assumption, statement, conclusion, etc. is true, safe, sufficient, and the like.
 1. Would that be a satisfactory way to measure humidity?
 2. Is that a safe argument?
 3. What about what the newspaper said on toll roads—is that true?

UTAH STUDY OF THE ASSESSMENT OF TEACHING

MARIE M. HUGHES
University of Utah

THE TITLE OF THIS PAPER CONTAINS A BIAS IN THE PURPOSE OF THE STUDY that grew out of the context in which the research was done. That context should be made explicit. The research was begun in January 1955, in a school district cooperating with the Utah State Committee on Merit Rating of Teachers. The grant of money to the cooperating districts was given with the charge to study the feasibility of and to formulate a method of rating teachers. Fortunately, the ways of working toward this objective were left entirely to the districts.

This context focused our attention directly on the instructional process.

The specific setting undoubtedly introduced an evaluative bias that affected the building of the instrument for the analysis of classroom teaching even though the research intent was *first* to describe teaching objectively as it was carried forward in the classroom.

A second influence on the research was a statement made by Barr in an article in which he summarized his studies and those of his students on measurement and prediction of teacher efficiency. These studies related grades, pattern of courses, and a long list of traits and characteristics to ratings of teaching efficiency. After his summary of the disappointing and inconsistent results of twenty years of work, he wrote: "Teaching effectiveness may be essentially a relationship between teachers, pupils and other persons directly concerned with the educational undertaking" [12, p. 174].* Such relationships could be described from data of classroom proceedings that focused on the interaction of teacher and student. We reasoned that the content of instruction was always mediated through the teacher. Moreover, the same records would make it possible to examine

* Numbers in brackets refer to items in the Bibliography, pp. 118–122.

the content for its accuracy, importance, suitability to age of student, or by any other criteria desired by the investigator.

The data of our study were classroom records obtained by two observers who checked with one another and collated their records. Most of the records were of thirty-minute duration. Thus a continuous sequential record of certain events occurring over a known period of time were secured. The "certain" or selected class of events were the teacher's verbal (nonverbal to the extent that it could be reliably obtained) behavior and the response of the child or group to whom the behavior was addressed.

Verbal behavior is, of course, the most continuous and pervasive of teacher behavior in the classroom. It has been designated by Mary Aschner as, "the language of responsible actions designed to influence the behavior of those under instruction" [8, p. 124].

There are many ways to analyze the records of actions in the classroom situation. The manner of analysis is controlled to a large degree by the definition accepted for teaching.

TEACHING DEFINED

A generic definition of teaching has been offered by Smith: "Teaching is a system of actions intended to induce learning" [53, p. 88]. Smith's definition makes it possible to examine the teacher's actions without reference to the learner since the "intent to induce learning" is sufficient. Smith's research has, in fact, analyzed teaching according to logical operations. These logical operations of teaching constitute 50 per cent of the verbal behavior of teachers in classes of English, social studies, science, and mathematics [53, p. 101].

A recent definition is offered by the American Educational Research Association (AERA) Committee on the *Handbook of Research on Teaching*. It defines teaching as a "form of interpersonal influence aimed at changing the behavior potential of another person" [24, p. 91].

To continue the explanation, "interpersonal influence" refers to behavior aimed at change in another." Also, "the teacher's behavior must gain its influence through being perceived by the learner" [24, p. 91].

The AERA Committee definition includes the learner and his perception of the teacher's behavior as necessary to his receiving the influence that might induce change in his behavior. On the other hand, the interpretation of teacher behavior that has influence includes the so-called "frozen behavior" of the teacher who wrote a book, prepared a film or a program for a teaching machine.

Whatever ambiguities may be located in this global definition of teaching, it is quite clear that the definition does accommodate the purpose of the undertaking the AERA Committee had in mind. It permits the inclusion in *The Handbook of Research on Teaching* of a very wide scope of phenomena related to education.

The purpose of the Utah research was to describe teaching and then evaluate it for the purpose of improving teaching. We were convinced that many years of research were necessary before merit rating could be done with objectivity and reliability.

The Utah investigations viewed the classroom as an involuntary group with goals roughly determined by the objectives of education. What was accepted as *good* teaching would be dependent on the major objectives accepted and the view of how these objectives could best be obtained. However, a description of teaching as it was in progress in the classroom could be secured by defining "teaching as interaction." Interaction is used in its dictionary sense of mutual or reciprocal action or influence. In other words the partners or objects in a situation act upon each other. Teaching, therefore, cannot be separated from the learner.

An element that is crucial in the classroom interactive situation is its nonequalitarian character. The teacher-student relationship is one of superior-subordinate. To take account of this ubiquitous element properly, the concept of *teacher power* influenced the building of the *Code for the Analysis of Teaching*[1] that was finally used to analyze the classroom records of teaching.

If we look again at the definition of teaching as interaction, we note that the influence is mutual or reciprocal; therefore, the degree to which the child or group in direct interaction with the teacher has influence must be traced out if a description of teaching defined as interaction is to be made. *Teacher responsiveness,* then, is the second concept to influence the building of the *Code*.

Before these two concepts—teacher power and teacher responsiveness—are discussed more fully, some additional framework must be made explicit to give full meaning to the accepted definition of teaching. It is assumed that the teacher's influence is directed toward some conscious end. That is, the teacher in the classroom has some purpose he has accepted which guides his influence attempts. Then intent to instruct or to aid the student in his learning may be assumed to be the purpose behind the teacher's effort to influence. On the other hand, the student's influence attempts are guided by his search for competence, his reach for his

---

[1] The complete title of this instrument is *The University of Utah Revision of the Provo Code for the Analysis of Teaching.*

own identity, and his defenses or protection of himself. The teacher's intent to instruct in such a manner as to change the behavior of the student and the student's response in terms of his own idiosyncratic system form the dynamics within which the interaction in the classroom takes place.[2]

It does imply a point of view regarding the nature of the learner and learning. It does accept the individuality of the learner, it sees him as active and purposeful in his influence attempts. It implies that he may be eager to accept as well as be resistant to teacher influence attempts. It categorically rejects the learner as passive, a receptacle to be filled, or an object responding mechanically to stimuli that is rewarded or punished.

These two major concepts of *teacher power* and *teacher responsiveness* to the influence of the student in the classroom situation are traced out in detail in the University Revision of the Provo *Code for the Analysis of Teaching*. The interpretation given these concepts in the definitions and content of the categories, used in the Provo *Code,* constitute the major differences between this *Code* and the other systems of categorizing classroom interaction.

THE CONCEPT OF TEACHER POWER

In the classroom interactive situation, the relationship is one of superior-subordinate. In this relationship, the teacher possesses a high power component. This power is derived from several sources; one is the age differential at least through elementary and secondary school. The chief source of power, however, is society sanctioned and legally bestowed. The teacher is a representative of the culture: there are commonly agreed-upon expectations that the teacher will do something to make the student learn, that he will present materials which the student ought to know. The most common expectation of what the student ought to know are the societal arts of reading, writing, and numbers. In broader terms we may say that the school is expected to cultivate the mind of the student.

The teacher has power, in contrast to the students, to arrange the learning environment, to decide the content to which attention is to be given, the standards that are to be maintained, and who is to do what. Also, the what and how of the distribution of rewards and punishments are the teacher's prerogative. In a very real sense, the students in the teacher-learner situation can do, with approval, only that which is permitted by the teacher.

The teacher's acts in the interactive situation carry a high potency,

[2] These dynamics were more fully described in an article entitled, "Teaching Is Interaction," *Elementary School Journal,* May 1958.

always with the latent power of punishment and even ultimate removal from the classroom and school. In other words, we believe that the teacher cannot act without exercising influence. Because this is so, the teacher's verbal and identifiable nonverbal behavior performs a *function* for the student or group in focus in the situation.

This interpretation of teacher influence appears to us to recognize the reality of the superior-subordinate relationship with the power component held by the teacher.

Getzels and Thelen, writing at a later time, expressed our point of view regarding teacher power somewhat dramatically:

> If one thinks of authority, control, and leadership in political terms, it is clear that the classroom group, at least in its formal aspects, is about as far from democracy as one can get. Not only do the students have no control over the selection of their leader, they normally also have no recourse from his leadership, no influence on his method of leadership beyond that granted by him, and no power over the tenure of his leadership. There are very few working groups in our society in which these essentially despotic conditions are legitimately so much the rule [29, p. 56].

In reading the transcripts of classroom interaction, we discovered that teachers exercised their power in quite different ways. We wished to describe these phenomena as carefully as possible, and thus our categories of control and imposition were formed with the use of subscripts to describe the degree of control.

THE CONCEPT OF TEACHER RESPONSIVENESS

When teaching is defined as interaction with its reciprocity between the actors in the situation, logic requires the tracing out of student influence in the classroom situation. Student influence can be known only through the teacher's response to what the student says and does.

The teacher responds by accepting, rejecting, and considering the student's statements or questions; by clarifying and elaborating on what the student has said. The teacher may approve or reprove the student. Requests are granted or refused. The work of the student is evaluated.

Since the student is viewed as the active agent in his own learning, his influence in the situation is shown by the teacher's response to what he has said or done and may be interpreted as his opportunity to exercise initiative and to develop his personal stake in the classroom activities.

Teacher responsiveness to the students' actions was traced out in the problem or work of the classroom under the category, *Development of Content*. Teacher responsiveness to the student as an individual with his own problems and activities unrelated to the work or content goal of the classroom was traced under the heading of *Personal Responsiveness*.

THE INSTRUMENT FOR ANALYSIS

If at this time investigators are offering a large number of classifications of teacher's verbal behavior, there are also many similarities. For example, teachers give directions of one kind or another. Most investigators tally such statements in a straightforward manner as directions. The reproof statements are categorized quite similarly from one investigator to another. In addition to similarities there are differences and, it is hoped, these differences may in time increase our insights regarding teaching. With any content analysis, the division of the material into the units for quantification is crucial.

Our unit of teacher behavior was the *function* performed for the group or student to whom the teacher was directing his influence. This function can be inferred from the context in which it occurred and does not necessarily conform to any conventional language unit. The validity of the inference is found in the content of the records. To analyze the records in this manner excludes a sampling technique of teacher verbal behavior since sequence of action and reaction is necessary to the process of inference. We are not unaware of the presumptuousness of this attempt, and we do share the concern of other investigators to describe teaching as objectively and as usefully as possible.

An example will indicate the difference between viewing the data as function (a construct) and recording it literally as my colleague, Dr. Travers, purports to do. I am using this episode with his permission. Under a general heading of informing he includes two smaller categories: ask questions and provide cues. A simple example will demonstrate the differences in coding:

CHILD: What is this word?
TEACHER: (covers up all but first two letters [th] of the word). What does this say?
CHILD: I don't know.
TEACHER: It is just the same as the letters say in *thin* (the word is things).
CHILD: There is an *ing*.

Do you code the first teacher act as a question or a cue? I submit that there is just as much logic for one point of view as another. In other words, the decision is made within the definition of the investigator and calls for judgment rather than literal translation. In the second teacher statement, there may be no argument about a cue being offered.

The University Revision of the Provo *Code* would view such teacher remarks as the first as that or re-structuring the attention of the student and designate it as *structure-invention*. It is reasoned that the teacher remains in control with the student expected to respond with correctness. The intent of the teacher to help neither ensures the success of the effort nor relieves the student from the desirability of knowing the correct response. Then there remains the interesting problem of, Did the teacher respond to the child's request for help or didn't he? Within our frame of reference, it is a more objective description to "tell the truth" and designate the action as *structure-intervention*. This says simply that the structure, whether made by a child or teacher, was shifted by the teacher. The same kind of problem presents itself in the second teacher statement when the teacher continues to ask the student a question. According to one analysis, he is structuring the student's attention. The teacher may be offering a cue with the intent of helping the student retrieve or locate the answer but intent is not the basis for analysis.

When the child asks the question and the teacher responds with a cue, has the teacher responded in the literal sense of the situation; or is the categorization of teacher behavior as cue more objectively descriptive because it escapes from the situation? When is the investigator analyzing in a manner that may be termed closest to the data of the teaching record?

Blake of Texas, in a paper originally circulated through the Office of Education Cooperative Research Branch, writes: "the most obvious need is for a development of a taxonomy and measurement technology of variables describing the stimulus situation."

Parsons and Shils present three independent variables in their theory of action: personality, social system, and culture. This suggests that the stimulus situation would be described independently and linked to the other variables through a series of constructs or mediating variables.

This short, tentative excursion into the problems of research in teaching is taken to suggest that the basic methodological problems have not been solved. We are a long way from either adequate conceptualization or the technology for measurement of the classroom situation. Some progress in conceptualization has been made as shown by a number of papers in the *Fifty-Ninth Yearbook, Part I, of the National Society for the Study of Education: Dynamics of Instructional Groups*.

In the meantime, the criteria against which a code for content analysis may be appraised are well established! It should be logical and consistent with independence of categories; reliability should be established, not only of the original workers but by other investigators removed from the original work. The simpler the method of analysis the more elegant it is. The framework and definitions within which the analysis is made, of necessity, govern the results; therefore, the results can be viewed as true or not true, useful or not useful, according to the acceptance of the framework and the degree to which the method of analysis meets the canons prescribed for such scientific endeavor.

ELABORATION OF THE UNIVERSITY CODE FOR THE ANALYSIS OF TEACHING, WITH SELECTED FINDINGS

We categorize teacher behavior under the seven broad categories of controlling, teacher imposition, facilitating, development of content, personal response, negative affectivity, and positive affectivity.

In our *Code* we attempted to trace out the manner in which control was exercised. We included in our definition of control the structuring of the problem or designation on the part of the teacher of the content to which the students are asked to give attention. The statement or statements doing this may be in question or declarative form. This act may be performed open or closed, depending on whether or not there is a single acceptable response.

The structure may be oriented to what has gone previously or it may be presented without reference to its antecedents. It may be done with public criteria, that is, the specific reason for the choice made public. Often these reasons give a linkage to cultural norms or values, or to a need evidenced by earlier performance on the part of students. Structure may be given in a self-oriented manner—"I want you to . . ." Structure may be an act of intervention that deflects the structure set up by the student or one in which the teacher changes his mind after setting it up for the students.

Regulate, another aspect of control, refers to the who and how. Again the regulation of who may be open (anyone), closed (person named); neutral (some agreed-upon procedure as around the circle, alphabetically, order of signing up, etc.), or global (leaving it open a few seconds and then designating). It may be closed, the person named, but with public criteria. In the same manner directions may be given with or without public criteria.

Standard setting and *judge* are other acts or functions performed under the broader category of *Controlling Functions.*

The use of the subscript of *public criteria* traces out the degree to which the teacher identifies the elements in the situation requiring certain behavior. Frequently, these elements (may be value factors) are the linkage between the school and the wider culture.

Public criteria, also, is a subscript affixed to acts of reproof and refusal of the student's request. The subscripts provide data on the teacher's manner of control which may then be interpreted as maximizing or minimizing the power component.

The category of *Development of Content* pertains to the problem or content goal of the student or group. This category traces out the teacher response to the student's activity with the content. We describe this as the teacher's response to the data the student places in the situation. These teacher responses are the accepting-clarifying statements. They are the answers to questions raised by the student. They are suggestions that the student go ahead and tell of his experience (structure turn back). Within this category are the teacher's remarks that point out other sources of information, other aspects of the problem, other ways of doing. The designation of *stimulate* is made when the teacher offers the material as alternatives without insisting that the student do it. The choice of doing must remain with the student. So far as our data are concerned, very few acts of stimulating were performed. The opportunity to do so was clear but most teacher's acts continued to press for some predetermined material.

Parenthetically, it is somewhat difcult to see how teaching can be improved with a few more subject-matter courses, while teacher behavior remains the same in the classroom.

Another aspect of *Development of Content* is that of evaluation ... defined with an unmistakable referent to content rather than a general "good," "O.K.," or "that's fine." When such statements are looked upon as reinforcement, one finds difficulty in apprehending what in the situation was reinforced, unless it was that the student responded when asked to do so by the teacher. By restricting the definition to a content referent, we at least know to what it refers. When the element or factor that made the work acceptable or nonacceptable is made specific, the subscript of discrimination is used.

Again it will be no surprise to indicate that few teachers evaluated with discrimination. Indeed, few teachers evaluated the student's performance in other than over-all support with "good," "O.K."—approval which is not our definition of evaluation. To the general expressed acceptance or approval we gave the designation support-stereotype.

The category of *Personal Response* traces out the interaction of teacher and student in situations wherein the content or problem structured by the teacher is not the focus of attention; instead, the interaction occurs because of something idiosyncratic with the student. He initiates the contact with the teacher, or his condition at the moment is such that the need for aid appears obvious; for example, a crying child trying to dial the telephone. That is, the teacher act is categorized here if she dialed the telephone for him. He could be responsible for touching the telephone. The mean percentage of teaching acts in this category was five. The mean for the three records of individual teachers varied from 2 per cent to 11 per cent with the mode at 4 per cent.

SUMMARY ON THE CODE

Since teaching was defined as interaction, student influence as well as teacher influence was traced out. The two chief concepts that undergirded the *Code* were those of Teacher Power and Teacher Responsiveness to student's actions.

The use of public criteria in relation to the teacher's action states that the reason for the teacher's action is made public. In most cases the teacher uses the cultural reality, including its conventions and values, for public criteria. When this is done, the teacher may be viewed as mediating the culture in a manner that provides a linkage between school and society.

ASSESSMENT OF TEACHING

The identification of teacher functions as defined by the *University Revision of the Provo Code* has demonstrated the wide repertoire of behavior open to the teacher. The fact that teachers actually use a small range of behavior may suggest a classroom program that is narrow and repetitive. The widest range of teaching behavior was found in the work or activity period. The narrowest range of teaching behavior was noted in the reading and arithmetic periods. More participation of students was apparent when the teacher used open structure with accepting, clarifying responses rather than closed structure.

Except for the ends of the distribution, teachers exhibited very much the same pattern of behavior. In other words, the differences found among teachers were contributed by relatively few individuals.

Teachers were somewhat more positive than negative in their behavior, although much of the positiveness was expressed in very general terms of support which we described as stereotyped.

The content under discussion received little elaboration. Students' questions, explorations, and personal experience were most frequently rebuffed or ignored. There was little attempt to build generalizations, to ask for comparisons, to look at alternatives, and to look at consequences. The process of analysis and synthesis was seldom demonstrated nor was the situation such that it could be interpreted as evoking these mental activities.

The most common situation was that of a teacher asking a question that was answered with the recall of a discrete item or fact.

Evaluation was done in such a general manner that the students were not helped to build finer discrimination or standards of work. Expanded criteria for evaluation are needed if this function is to contribute to greater intellectual development of students. Smith's work is very suggestive here.

The act of *stimulating,* defined as opening the field for the student through the introduction of additional sources of information, of other facets for exploration, and of other activities that could be initiated, was seldom performed.

Research is needed to continue to test the patterns or syndromes of teaching acts for their effects.

What patterns of teaching acts aid a student in developing confidence and independence?

What patterns of teaching acts help a student to become involved in content or subject matter for the reward it gives him or because he views it as instrumental to a larger goal he has?

What patterns of teaching acts help the student remain open to experience, to continue to be a learner?

What patterns of teaching acts aid the student in his development of responsible self-discipline that contributes to personal and socially desirable productivity?

What patterns of teaching acts foster the student's creativity?

What patterns of teaching acts help the student to develop his entire range of intellectual and emotional capacities?

What patterns of teaching acts help the student become a "caring" individual?

It is obvious that these questions reflect some of my own values that may be expressed as objectives of education.

The teacher who becomes aware of the effects of his behavior is in a position to change it. Competence that may be considered uniquely that of a teacher may lie in the ability to discriminate the nature of the structure as process and also as content. Competence will also be displayed in the ability to respond to the data generated by the actions and reactions of the students.

Such professional abilities appear necessary if the classroom is to offer a more meaningful reality-centered situation for the student.

METHODOLOGICAL NOTES

The increased use of transcriptions of classroom proceedings as the basic data for the study of teaching is most encouraging. The expense and time involved is considerable, and even these data do not obtain all the useful data; for example, the activities of the students not in direct interaction with the teacher. To illustrate, a kindergarten teacher, whose interactions were very negative, gave the children much freedom on their own so long as they were reasonably behaved. This was a unique situation. Perhaps each class is more unique than the quantified data show.

TEACHER INFLUENCE IN THE CLASSROOM

NED A. FLANDERS
University of Michigan

THE PRESENT ARTICLE IS THE FIRST OF A SERIES REPORTING RESEARCH on the teacher's influence in the classroom. The general purpose of the series is to develop tentative principles of teacher influence that some day may contribute to a theory of classroom instruction. A theory of instruction would be broader in scope than a theory of learning and would involve concepts describing both the pupil's and teacher's behavior. Such a theory would be quite apart from the various subjects taught and would be concerned with the effects of the teacher's behavior on motivation and attitude formation. This first article begins with a review of research on classroom climate and then presents tentative hypotheses of teacher influence.

Most of the research reviewed in this article makes use of observational techniques to assess the spontaneous behavior of the teacher. The analysis of spontaneous teacher behavior involves the development and standardization of a system of categories that an observer can use to note the frequency of qualitatively different acts. Systematic observation produces a frequency distribution within discrete categories that can be drawn as a histogram profile covering short or long periods of observation. Profiles from long periods of observation ignore variability of teacher influence that is easily seen if profiles of the same teacher over short time periods are compared.

The ultimate goal of studying teacher influence in the classroom is to understand teacher-pupil interaction and, in particular, to specify conditions in which learning is maximized. The research on classroom climate that is reviewed in the next section contributes to a general understanding of teacher influence over long time periods, but ignores short-term influence patterns of the teacher and changes in classroom conditions that occur as a result of learning.

RESEARCH ON CLASSROOM CLIMATE

The words "classroom climate" refer to generalized attitudes toward the teacher and the class that the pupils share in common in spite of individual differences. The development of these attitudes is an outgrowth of classroom social interaction. As a result of participating in classroom activities, pupils soon develop shared expectations about how the teacher will act, what kind of person he is, and how they like their class. These expectations color all aspects of classroom behavior creating a social atmosphere or climate that appears to be fairly stable, once established. Thus the word *climate*[1] is merely a shorthand reference to those qualities that consistently predominate in most teacher-pupil contacts and contacts between pupils in the presence or absence of the teacher.

The earliest systematic studies of spontaneous pupil and teacher behavior that relate directly to classroom climate are those of H. H. Anderson and his colleagues, Helen and Joseph Brewer and Mary Francis Reed [2, 3, 4, 5], and are based on the observation of "dominative" and "integrative" contacts. It is essential to understand the qualitative differences between an integrative and a dominative social contact because most of the research on classroom climate makes similar behavioral distinctions.

A preliminary study showed that it was possible to devise reliable measures of behavior of young children. Behavior was recorded as "Contacts" and divided into two groups of categories. If a child snatched a toy, struck a playmate, or commanded him, or if he attempted to force him in some way, such contacts were included under the term "domination." By such behavior he ignored the rights of the companion; he tended to reduce the free interplay of differences and to lead toward resistance or conformity in responding or adapting to another.

Other contacts were recorded which tended to increase the interplay of differences. Offering a companion a choice or soliciting an expression of his desires were gestures of flexibility and adaptation. These tended in the

---

[1] Climate is assessed either by analyzing teacher-pupil interaction—and inferring underlying attitudes—or by the use of a pupil attitude inventory, and predicting the quality of classroom interaction. Its precise meaning, when commonly used, is seldom clear, just as its synonyms "morale," "rapport," and "emotional tone" are also ambiguous. To have any meaning at all, the word is always qualified by an adjective and it is in the choice of adjectives that researchers confuse objectivity; e.g., Lippitt and White's choice of "authoritarian" and "democratic" to describe climate. "Direct" and "indirect" have difficulties also. In later articles the word "climate" will not be used; it is used in the present article because it appeared in the research being reviewed.

direction of discovering common purposes among differences. Such contacts were grouped under the term "socially integrative behavior" [5, p. 12].

The findings of Anderson *et al.* are based on the study of preschool, primary, and elementary school classrooms involving several different teachers and extending over several years. Taken altogether, their imaginative research has produced a series of internally consistent and significant findings. First, the dominative and integrative contacts of the teacher set a pattern of behavior that spreads throughout the classroom; the behavior of the teacher, more than any other individual, sets the climate of the class. The rule is that when either type of contact predominates, domination incites further domination, and integration stimulates further integration. It is the teacher's tendency that spreads among pupils even when the teacher is no longer in the room. Furthermore, the pattern a teacher develops in one year is likely to persist in his classroom the following year with completely different pupils. Second, when a teacher has a higher proportion of integrative contacts, pupils show more spontaneity and initiative, voluntary social contributions, and acts of problem solving. Third, when a teacher has a higher proportion of dominative contacts, the pupils are more easily distracted from schoolwork, and show greater compliance to, as well as rejection of, teacher domination.

A year or so after Anderson started his work, Lippitt and White [40], working with Kurt Lewin, carried out laboratory experiments to analyze the effects of adult leaders' influence on boys' groups. The laboratory approach used had certain advantages (or disadvantages, depending on your point of view) in studying the effects of the adult leader's behavior: The contrasting patterns of leader behavior were purified and made more consistent as a result of training and role playing; differences in the underlying personality and appearances of the adult leaders were minimized through role rotation; and the effect of the pattern of leader behavior was intensified, compared to a classroom, since there were only five boys to a group. Roughly speaking, the pattern Lippitt and White named "authoritarian leadership" consisted of dominative contacts; "democratic leadership" consisted of integrative contacts; and "laissez-faire leadership" consisted of irregular and infrequent integrative contacts with an element of indifference to the total group that is seldom found in a classroom and was not present in the Anderson *et al.* studies.

Most of the conclusions of the Lippitt and White study confirm or extend the general conclusions of Anderson *et al.* with some semantic modification but very little change, if any, in behavioral meaning. From the point of view of classroom teaching one interesting extension was the conceptualization of "dependence on the leader" by Lippitt and White.

This is a state of affairs in which group members were unable to proceed without directions from the leader. Anderson *et al.* used the category "conforming to teacher domination" and thus noted its occurrence, but in the more concentrated social climates of the laboratory experiments it was clearly seen that extensive compliance occurs when there is a generalized condition of dependence.

As a result of these two basic and independent studies that produced mutually supportive results, the notion of social climate was established. Additional research revealed minor variations of the central theme already established. Withall [58] showed that a simple classification of the teacher's verbal statements into seven categories produced an index of teacher behavior almost identical to the integrative-dominative (I-D) ratio of Anderson *et al.* Flanders [21] created laboratory situations in which contrasting patterns of teacher behavior were exposed to one pupil at a time. A sustained dominative pattern was consistently disliked by pupils, reduced their ability to recall, later on, the material studied, and produced disruptive anxiety as indicated by galvanic skin response and changes in the heartbeat rates. The reverse trends were noted as pupil reactions to integrative contacts. Perkins [48], using Withall's technique, studied groups of teachers organized to study the topic of child growth and development. He found that greater learning about child growth and development occurred when group discussion was free to focus on that topic; groups with an integrative type of leader were able to do this more frequently than were groups lead by a dominative type of leader. In a large cross-sectional study that did not use observation of spontaneous teacher behavior, Cogan [18] administered a single paper-and-pencil instrument to 987 eighth-grade students in thirty-three classrooms that contained three scales: a scale assessing student perceptions of the teachers, a scale on which students reported how often they did required schoolwork, and a scale on which students reported how often they did extra, nonrequired schoolwork. Cogan's first scale assessed traits one would associate with the behavior patterns observed in the research already cited although it was developed in terms of Murray's list of major personality needs [18, p. 326]. The items of one pattern were grouped as "dominative," "aggressive," and "rejectant"; in the other pattern were "integrative," "affiliative," and "nurturant." These correspond to Anderson's dominative and integrative patterns. Cogan found that students reported doing more assigned and extra schoolwork when they perceived the teacher's behavior as falling into the integrative pattern rather than the dominative pattern.

Altogether these research projects support the statements about classroom climate that appear in the first paragraph of this section. The

Teacher Influence in the Classroom

two teacher behavior patterns[2] that create the contrasting classroom climates have been well established.

THE INTEGRATIVE PATTERN	THE DOMINATIVE PATTERN
a. accepts, clarifies, and supports the ideas and feeling of pupils	a. expresses or lectures about own ideas or knowledge
b. praises and encourages	b. gives directions or orders
c. asks questions to stimulate pupil participation in decision making	c. criticizes or deprecates pupil behavior with intent to change it
d. asks questions to orient pupils to schoolwork	d. justifies his own position or authority

Associated Attitudes of Teacher (suggested by Cogan)

outgoing	patient	antisocial	impatient
good-natured	self-effacing	surly	self-centered
friendly	self-submissive	spiteful	self-assertive
cheerful	responsive	dour	aloof
trustful		hostile	

These research results should be interpreted with caution. They do not suggest that there is a single pattern of teacher behavior that should be continually maintained in the classroom. Anyone with teaching experience recognizes that there are situations in which an integrative teacher behavior pattern is less appropriate than a dominative pattern; furthermore, it is possible that identical acts by the teacher may in one situation be perceived by pupils as dominative and in another situation as integrative. These research results do show that over a period of time, more integrative than dominative teacher-pupil contacts will establish desirable pupil attitudes and superior patterns of work. The work of Anderson *et al.* and Cogan presents evidence that a desirable climate results in more learning, although additional evidence is needed to confirm the conclusion.

THE IMPLICATION OF RESEARCH ON CLASSROOM CLIMATE FOR A THEORY OF INSTRUCTION

Research on classroom climate is incomplete because it does not contribute to the question, "Why and when should a teacher react in either a

---

[2] Most of the researchers cited have their own favorite words to describe essentially the same behavior patterns. Anderson *et al.*: "dominative vs. integrative"; Lippitt and White: "authoritarian vs. democratic vs. laissez-faire"; Withall, Flanders, Perkins: "teacher-centered vs. student-centered"; and Cogan: "preclusive vs. inclusive." For the sake of simplicity, Anderson's terms have been used in the first section of this paper; the concepts "direct influence" and "indirect influence" will be introduced later.

dominative or integrative manner?" An adequate theory of instruction should specify the effects of integrative or dominative contacts for different types of situations that occur frequently in the classroom. Stated another way, there is a need for a dynamic explanation of how short-term patterns of teacher influence affect momentary situations so that the flexibility of the teacher's behavior is taken into account.

One clue that supports the notion that teachers probably are flexible in exerting dominative and integrative influences over short periods of time appears in the work of Mitzel and Rabinowitz [45] who used Withall's technique to assess the classroom climate of four teachers. Their observation data were organized to permit an analysis of variance between teachers, visits, and observers. Since the median length of an observer's visit was of the order of twenty minutes, the finding of statistically significant, wide variability among visits for the same teacher suggests that teachers adapt their influence to the immediate situation. There may be several reasons for the flexibility of teacher influence.

Teachers may adapt their influence to fit different phases of problem solving that probably occur in the classroom. Bales and Strodtbeck [10] have found that the quality of verbal interaction changes, in group problem-solving discussion, as the discussion progresses through phases of orientation, evaluation, and control.

Teachers may also adapt their influence to fit the needs of the individual pupil in contacts with single pupils. In two different studies involving college-age students, Wispe [57] and Smith [51] have shown that psychologically different types of students, identified by personality tests, have different reactions to the same teacher behavior patterns. This was equally true of the two contrasting patterns used in each study and while the patterns were by no means identical to Anderson's dominative-integrative contrast, they were in many ways similar. Gage [25], in a study of elementary school children, found that pupils' perceptions of the same teacher were different according to whether the pupil could be classified as tending to seek "affective" or "cognitive" responses from a teacher.

Even though research on climate tends to ignore flexibility of teacher influence and is restricted to generalized, broad patterns of teacher behavior, it does make a fundamental contribution to a theory of instruction. This contribution consists of identifying general patterns of the teacher influence that produce predictable responses of pupils and thus establishes cause-and-effect principles that are true in the long run. However, the task of investigating flexibility of influence remains uninvestigated.

TENTATIVE HYPOTHESES OF TEACHER INFLUENCE

The purpose of this section is to develop hypotheses of teacher influence that are consistent with generalizations about classroom climate but which also account for flexibility of teacher influence. Most of the hypotheses are not yet supported by research evidence. If future experimentation provides evidence in support of the hypotheses, they may contribute to a theory of instructions.[3]

In the classroom teacher-pupil relationships are essentially superior-subordinate in quality. The responsibility for classroom activities is the teacher's and both the teacher and the pupils expect the teacher to take charge, to initiate and to control the learning activities. The freedom to direct or not to direct the activities of others is initially given only to the teacher; whatever freedom pupils have in this respect results from the actions of the teacher. No pupil can consistently ignore the authority of the teacher and it is most difficult and sometimes impossible for a pupil to escape from the teacher's control. In the discussion that follows, the word *dependence* will be used to refer to these essential qualities of a superior-subordinate relationship. The presence of dependence has already been noted in the work of Anderson and Lippitt and White.

The opposite of dependence is *independence* and since various degrees of dependence or independence exist, they must be distinguished in the discussion that follows. *High dependence* will refer to a condition in which pupils voluntarily seek additional ways of complying to the authority of the teacher. This condition has aptly been described by Lewin [38, p. 132] as, "at every point within his [the pupil's] sphere of action he is internally controlled by the wishes of the adult [teacher]." He adds, later, that a pupil might even anticipate these wishes. *Medium dependence* will refer to the average classroom condition in which teacher direction is essential to initiate and guide activities but the pupils do not voluntarily solicit it. When it occurs they comply. *Low dependence* refers to a condition in which pupils would react to teacher directions if they occurred but their present activities, usually teacher initiated, can be carried on without continued teacher direction. In the face of difficulties pupils would prefer the teacher's help. *Independence* refers to a condition in which the pupils perceive their activities to be "self-directed" (even though the teacher may have helped create the perception) and they do not expect

---

[3] For an initial consideration of a "theory of instruction" the author is indebted to Professor Herbert A. Thelen, University of Chicago; see "Toward a Theory of Instruction," *J. of Ed. Res.*, October 1951 (entire issue).

directions from the teacher. In the face of difficulties pupils would prefer at least to try their own solutions before seeking the teacher's help. If teacher direction is given, pupils would feel free to evaluate it in terms of the requirements of the learning activities.

Underlying the entire discussion that follows is the basic assumption that the learning potential of pupils is inversely related to their level of dependence within reasonable and practical limits of classroom organization. In a condition of high dependence a pupil is too concerned with his relationship to the teacher to be completely objective about the learning task. "Objectivity cannot arise in a constraint situation; it arises only in a situation of freedom" [38, p. 178]. No doubt there are philosophical values at issue here, but it is psychologically sound and logically self-evident to point out that the learning experience is distorted to the extent that the dependence present in the learning situation is not present in the situation in which the learning is applied. No pupil is ever completely independent of the teacher's authority, nor is anyone completely independent in society, but there are certain types of desirable educational objectives that can be achieved only in a situation involving the degree of independence defined in the preceding paragraph. It is equally true that there are some limited objectives that can best be achieved in a condition of medium dependence, also defined above.

Conditions of dependence or independence are created by the teacher's choice of influence. One can conceive of *direct influence* and *indirect influence* which, under appropriate circumstances, determine the degree of dependence. These two kinds of influence can be defined in terms of verbal behavior, as follows:

Direct Influence consists of stating the teacher's own opinions or ideas, directing the pupil's action, criticizing his behavior, or justifying the teacher's authority or use of that authority.

Indirect Influence consists of soliciting the opinions or ideas of the pupils, applying or enlarging on the opinions or ideas of the pupils, praising or encouraging the participation of pupils, or clarifying and accepting the feelings of pupils.

It will be shown in later articles that the teacher's direct and indirect influence can be reliably assessed by observation in spontaneous classroom situations and that the dependence of pupils can also be assessed by observation or paper-and-pencil techniques.

If the flexibility of teacher influence is to be understood, a theory of teacher influence should explain why direct influence may, in one situation, increase or maintain dependence, and in another situation, may increase or maintain independence. The cues used consciously or unconsciously by a teacher to guide his choice of influence may arise from *Gestalten* so complex as to defy conceptualization. In order to be parsimonious, the theory about to be conceptualized will employ the fewest number of variables that seem necessary to predict and understand the teacher's choice of influence.

One aspect of the classroom situation that should make a difference in the pupil's reaction to teacher influence is his perception of the learning goal and the methods of reaching that goal. One can conceive of a situation in which the goal and the methods of reaching it are clear to the pupil and another situation in which these are unclear. Certainly the reactions of a student to teacher influence when he knows what he is doing and when he is not sure of what he is doing will be different. In the discussion that follows, reference will be made to clear goals and unclear goals in order to distinguish between these two situations.

Another aspect of the goal in a learning situation is whether or not the goal is perceived by the student as desirable or undesirable. The attraction of a goal determines motivation[4] and this attribute of a goal has been designated by Lewin [38, p. 77] as *positive valence* or *negative valence*. In the discussion that follows, a positive valence is assigned to goals that satisfy the interests of pupils AND require goal activities that match their abilities. A negative valence is assigned to goals that fail to satisfy the interests of pupils AND/OR require activities that do not match their abilities.

By logical convention, an unclear goal has an unknown or neutral valence.

It should now be clear that the theory about to be developed will suggest that direct and indirect influence will have a different but predictable effect in situations where (*a*) the goal is unclear, (*b*) the goal is clear with a positive valence, and (*c*) the goal is clear with a negative valence. The operational differences between these three situations, necessary for experimentation, are (*a*) the pupils do not know what goal will develop, (*b*) the pupils know what the goal is, know what steps they will take to reach the goal, see necessary actions as matching their ability, and are very interested and satisfied to be working toward that goal, and (*c*) the pupils know what the goal is, what steps are necessary to reach the goal, may or may not see necessary actions as matching their ability, and are very uninterested and dissatisfied to be working toward that goal.

[4] Whether one refers to motivation as a "drive toward" or an "attraction to" a goal is irrelevant to the present discussion.

SITUATIONS IN WHICH GOALS ARE UNCLEAR

Suppose one assumes that:

Assumption A: There exists a drive in both the teacher and the pupils to establish a learning goal in the classroom and to work toward that goal.

Assumption B: When the goal is unclear, the behavior of pupils participating in identifying and clarifying a goal is determined by the real or imagined restraints of the teacher's control.

This is to say that most pupils expect to work on "schoolwork" in the classroom; that in order to get started, they expect the teacher to initiate activities that will clarify a learning goal and spell out the steps required to reach the goal. In short there exists in a classroom with unclear goals, a state of medium dependency.

NOTE: H refers to hypothesis; SH to subhypothesis.

H 1.00 Indirect influence increases independence, when goals are unclear, by reducing the real or imagined restraints[5] of the teacher's control.

    SH 1.10 When restraints are at the barest minimum needed to coordinate class activity, pupils will have the maximum opportunity to express their interests in the goals suggested and to compare their abilities with the activities required.

    SH 1.20 Pupils who tend to be uncomfortable with minimum teacher restraints will need considerable support and encouragement, as part of the teacher's indirect influence, in order to continue to express their interests and to compare their abilities.

These hypotheses suggest that the effect of indirect influence, when goals are unclear, is to stimulate the expression of the pupil's interest, curiosity, and appreciation of several possible learning goals and to evaluate these goals in terms of the methods required to reach them. To be realistic, the goal requirements should be within range of the abilities of the pupils. During this activity the teacher takes an active part by asking questions, praising and encouraging pupil participation, and expressing his own opinions primarily in terms of pupil ideas. In practice, the more

---

[5] "Restraints" is a word originally used by Lewin to refer to barriers. Here it refers to barriers the teacher sets to pupils' behavior or that pupils imagine that the teacher sets. Included would be prohibitions, admonitions, and imposed directions. The author recognizes that every teacher must set "minimum restraints," but he believes that if they are set reasonably, pupils will perceive a degree of freedom that permits disciplined self-direction. Technically, restraints refer to forces which exist in the pupil's social environment (life space).

mature judgment of the teacher is expressed by what he chooses to praise and the particular ideas he chooses to question or develop.

- H 2.00 Direct influence increases dependence, when goals are unclear, by maintaining or increasing the restraints of the teacher's control.
  - SH 2.10 With high dependence or increasing medium dependence, direct influence results in overt compliance.
  - SH 2.11 If the goals subsequently prove interesting and match the pupil's ability, the overt compliance will occur with inner acceptance.
  - SH 2.12 If goals subsequently prove uninteresting or do not match the pupil's ability, the overt compliance will occur with inner resistance.
  - SH 2.13 Either type of compliance maintains the restraints of the teacher's control and pupils will be more dependent throughout the entire process of reaching the goal, compared to goals identified with indirect influence.
    - SH 2.20 Pupils who are more comfortable in a dependent teacher relationship will actively solicit the teacher's direct influence when goals are unclear.

These hypotheses suggest that the effect of direct influence, when goals are unclear, is to increase, or at least maintain, the existing dependence of pupils on the teacher's control. Under these circumstances, direct influence restricts the alternative reactions of pupils to overt compliance. Festinger [50] has suggested that public compliance to group pressures can occur with private acceptance or without private acceptance; with a slight change in words, his analysis is adapted here as a reasonable outcome of direct influence. The notion that either type of compliance maintains a dependent relationship is, perhaps, most questionable in the case of overt compliance with inner acceptance. However, it can be argued that compliance is less a matter of working on an interesting or uninteresting goal, and due more to a perception of the pupil that he must work on that goal only, if he is to receive the approval of the teacher who holds ultimate authority. The consequences of this perception will be discussed later.

Both SH 1.20 and SH 2.20 are tentative extensions of the work of Wispe, Smith and Gage, whose studies of individual pupil reactions to various types of teacher influence have already been mentioned.

The hypotheses stated are presumed to hold whenever goals are unclear either for individual pupils or for the class as a whole, whether this occurs at the beginning, middle, or near the end of a particular learning cycle. Goals are most likely to be unclear for the total class during the initial phases of a learning cycle. However, it is a common experience to be working toward what appears to be a clear goal only to find, after some progress, that the original picture of the goal has become unrealistic. Barriers to progress lower goal clarity by changing the steps required to reach the goal. The incidence of unclear goal perceptions among pupils may be far more frequent at the beginning of a school year when pupils, teacher, subject, and methods are less understood. In general, unclear goals become clear with the passage of time, either suddenly or gradually, if efforts to reach the goal are maintained. Since perceptions of the goal are subject to individual differences and some goals are more difficult to understand than others, a teacher must assume that there is a range of goal perceptions in a class at any given moment.

The development of positive or negative valence occurs simultaneously with the clarification of goals and methods of reaching goals. As soon as a pupil imagines a relationship between his interests and abilities and the nature of a goal, positive or negative valence is anticipated. Many pupils bring into the classroom a generalized anticipation of goal valence based on past experience, the previous class, or their attitudes toward the teacher. Indirect influence is particularly useful for clarifying such feelings and relating them to the present goal activities.

In the next two sections consideration is given to situations in which the goal and the goal activities are sufficiently clear for pupils to have definite positive or negative reactions toward the goal. But before these situations are discussed, it is necessary to examine more closely the meaning of dependence and independence when goals are clear.

As a goal becomes clear with a positive valence, a force toward the goal develops, action becomes rewarding, and the resultant pupil behavior is usually classified as "self-motivated." As a goal becomes clear with a negative valence, a force away from the goal develops, action becomes unrewarding, and if the resultant pupil behavior is oriented toward the goal, it is usually the result of a force created by the teacher through the use of reward or punishment. In this latter situation medium or high dependence exists and pupils comply with forces that stem from the teacher's authority. In the case of a clear, positive goal dependence exists to the extent that the pupil reacts, either consciously or unconsciously, to forces that stem from the teacher's authority. This latter case is most clearly illustrated by the pupil who senses that his present enjoyment in working on a rewarding task is a "gift" or is permitted by the teacher. He expresses his dependence by appreciating the teacher as well as the nature of the task. In a practical problem-solving sense, his objectivity is distorted since his decisions include judgments of what the teacher will

Teacher Influence in the Classroom

approve or disapprove, as well as the more objective requirements of the problem. His behavior is the resultant of both the restraining forces set by the teacher and the force that results from the positive goal valence.

SITUATIONS IN WHICH THE GOAL IS CLEAR WITH A POSITIVE VALENCE

With a clear, positive goal there is a strong force toward the goal which will be stable as long as the action satisfies the pupil's interests and his ability permits him to proceed. If the restraining forces set by the teacher are small, compared with the valence force, the pupil's behavior will be relatively independent. If the restraining forces approach significance, compared with the valence force, the dependence of the pupil will increase. The proportional balance of these two sets of forces depends on the use of direct or indirect influence when the goals are initially clarified and on subsequent influence that the teacher provides.

H 3.00   When the initial positive valence of a goal is clarified with indirect influence, the effect of subsequent direct or indirect influence on the existing independence is insignificant.

    SH 3.10   The tendency of subsequent direct influence to increase dependence, and indirect influence to decrease it, is greater when the influence is initiated by the teacher, compared with being solicited by pupils.

        SH 3.20   Independent progress toward a clear, positive goal re-enforces the valence and provides pupils with objective criteria with which to evaluate teacher influence.

These hypotheses emphasize the primary goal orientation of an independent pupil moving successfully toward a clear, positive goal. Teacher influence solicited by pupils is likely to have a goal orientation and, as such, will not affect independence. Influence initiated by the teacher is unlikely to affect independence unless the pupil fails to see a relationship between such influence and the goal; e.g., when the teacher attempts to change to a completely different goal. Given conditions which include maximum independent goal orientation and minimum teacher's restraints, barriers to progress are more likely to appear as an intellectual challenge. With proper teacher stimulation and direct challenge there would be an opportunity to enrich the problem-solving experience by stretching the goal requirements to the limit of pupil ability, without loss of positive valence.

In the case of a clear goal with a positive valence that was developed with direct influence, the restraining forces set by the teacher would be of sufficient magnitude to affect the pupil's behavior. However, successful progress toward a positive goal may modify the original dependence. This modification is probably due to the development of the valence force and not due to a decrease in the restraining forces; on this point, however, there is certainly the possibility of different interpretations. Lewin [38, p. 169] would suggest that the decrease in restraining forces would be more likely to occur with younger children, providing the goal activities are truly rewarding. With older children, the realization that the original direct influence was, in a sense, unjustified would increase the pupil's awareness of the restraining forces. Although the dynamics of this situation are not yet clear, the author is disposed to suggest the following hypotheses primarily because dependence is easier to create, during initial stages, than it is to diminish, in later stages.

    H 4.00   When the initial positive valence of a goal is clarified with direct influence, subsequent direct influence maintains or increases existing dependence and subsequent indirect influence decreases existing dependence only slightly, if at all.

        SH 4.10   If a goal that is initiated with direct influence develops a positive valence, the existing dependence of the pupils is re-enforced by the rewarding experience.

            SH 4.20   Direct influence during initial clarification of positive goals, followed by indirect influence, maintains existing dependence if pupils become aware of the inconsistency in the teacher's influence.

These hypotheses suggest, in effect, that once dependence is established, under conditions of H 2.00, it is not likely to decrease even if the learning goal develops a positive valence.

SITUATIONS IN WHICH THE GOAL IS CLEAR WITH A NEGATIVE VALENCE

In this situation the actions of both the teacher and pupils are limited. The teacher usually attempts to maintain the restricted learning possibilities by exerting direct influence through either reward or punishment. The only other alternative is to attempt to change the valence of the goal. This second alternative will be considered first.

Dislike of a goal or of the activities required to reach a goal depends on the total perceptual field of the pupil. He may think the task is too difficult, too tedious, of no future value, or he may simply dislike the teacher. The reorganization of the pupil's perceptual field is best facilitated by indirect influence that clarifies and supports the pupil's diagnosis of his own difficulties. Successfully carried out, the process is very similar to initiating a new goal. A resourceful teacher recognizes that it is the pupil's perception that must be changed, that only he can change it, and that the change can often occur with only minor alterations in the nature of the goal or goal activities. In fact, the same task, imbedded in a different perceptual organization, may take on a completely different valence [38, p. 168].

H 5.00   A shift from negative to positive goal valence is most likely to occur in response to indirect influence by the teacher.

The analysis of situations involving reward and punishment has already been carried out by Lewin [38, pp. 114–170] and an analysis of complaint behavior has been published by Festinger [50, pp. 232–256]. In both references there are many principles which apply directly to the classroom and are related to direct influence, compliance, and dependence. In nearly every classroom, reward or punishment is never used alone; instead, the two are used in combination. The essence of direct influence with the threat of punishment or possibility of reward is the creation of a conflict situation which restricts the pupil's freedom and narrows the alternative actions of the pupil to one or two that the teacher desires. The maintenance of these restrictions requires alert and active surveillance of pupil behavior by the teacher because there are usually a few pupils who are willing and able to test the limits of their freedom in imaginative and unusual ways. With negative goal valence, if the threat of punishment is relaxed or if rewards are unfulfilled, action toward the goal decreases or stops. Thus, high dependence is maintained at all times.

SUMMARY AND CONCLUSIONS

The major purpose in reviewing research on classroom climate and in developing hypotheses about the effects of direct and indirect teacher influence is to explain variability of teacher influence. In considering, first, situations in which goals are unclear, and second, situations in which goals are clear, different effects of the same teacher behavior were hypothesized. Subsequent articles will be concerned with testing these hypotheses in either field studies or laboratory experiments.

A general assumption underlying the discussion is that there are times when direct influence and other times when indirect influence is most appropriate in the control of classroom learning. At first glance, this assumption may appear to conflict with the findings of research on classroom climate. However, a careful study of the data collected indicates that in all types of classroom situations both direct and indirect influence occurred. A widespread misinterpretation of research on classroom climate has been that direct influence should be avoided in the classroom. H 3.00 suggests that there will be no change in dependence when direct influence is exerted during periods when goals are clear. In fact, direct influence related to a clear goal may provide opportunities to challenge the ideas and conclusions of the pupil and to enrich the learning process.

The contrast between predictions of H 1.00 and H 2.00 with those of H 3.00 provides a tentative explanation of why direct or indirect influence may in one situation have one outcome, and in another situation a different outcome.

Many factors have been ignored in this initial statement of teacher influence. Some data have already been collected (and will be reported later) suggesting that younger pupils, ages five through seven, do not react to direct influence in the same way as older pupils. If this trend is supported some modification of H 1.00 and H 2.00 will be required that takes into account the age of the pupils. Data from the classroom of older pupils also suggests that certain kinds of learning activities can be introduced into classrooms with what appears to be almost instantaneous goal clarity. If this is true, such activities may be unrelated to H 1.00 and H 2.00. Data from high school classes suggest that certain topics such as mathematics and science are normally associated with a higher proportion of direct influence although, at the moment, this should be considered as no more than a commentary on current school practice.

No effort has been made in the present article to indicate how patterns of direct influence can be modified by using group activities in the classroom. It may be that the teacher who uses group methods can control dependence by making appropriate shifts in the classroom organization. Finally, there are certain obvious relationships between the hypotheses of teacher influence, principles of counseling, and the trainer's role in group therapy that have not been developed.

THE ANALYSIS OF VERBAL INTERACTION IN THE CLASSROOM

MARY JANE McCUE ASCHNER
Center for Cognitive Studies
Harvard University

TEACHING STUDIED "IN SITU"—WHYS AND WHEREFORES

THANKS TO SUCH PIONEERING STUDIES AS THOSE CARRIED OUT BY HUGHES [34], Flanders [22], Smith [55, 54], and others, it is no longer necessary to urge the importance of the classroom as the site of fruitful research into the nature and conduct of the teaching process. If our purpose is to upgrade the quality of the education that our schools provide, then one focal point of concern for educational theory and research is the quality of teaching done in school, in the classroom.

The effectiveness of teaching is measured, ultimately, in the success or failure of the student to grasp and master what his teacher is trying to transmit to him through instruction. But since the student himself is equally with the teacher the agent of his own learning processes—hence of his own success or failure to learn—it is not logically possible, in a given case, to evaluate the teaching that was done solely in terms of the learner's achievement. Consequently, it is necessary not only to study the conduct of teaching as it goes on moment by moment in the classroom; it is also necessary to study the behaviors of students during and under instruction. In this way some beginnings have been made, in tracing relationships between what teachers and students do and say in the transactions of classroom instruction, and the learning outcomes issuing from these transactions.

With the advent of the tape recorder and the development of adequate observation and transcription procedures, a vast store of data has begun to accumulate in the form of class session "tapescripts." Since 1957, on the Smith [55] and the Gallagher-Aschner [27] projects alone, we now have a total of 235 full-session tapescripts, representing nine Illinois schools, grades seven through twelve, forty-eight class groups at various ability levels, with forty-three teachers, over the content areas of English, social studies, mathematics, and science. In the study of such protocol materials, the techniques of teaching and the responding behaviors of students can be brought down to "slow motion" for analysis from any number of standpoints In the remainder of this paper, I shall present some of the standpoints from which these data have been analyzed with respect to the classroom behaviors of intellectually gifted boys and girls.

A CATEGORY SYSTEM FOR CLASSIFYING VERBAL BEHAVIORS[1]

This report outlines the development of a Category System for classifying the thought processes that are reflected in verbal behavior, in the context of group discussion. It is being used in an attempt to describe the amount and quality of productive thinking that gifted children do during sequences of class discussion at the junior high school level. In September 1959, a four-year longitudinal study of gifted children was initiated with a pilot project by Professor J. J. Gallagher and myself, at the Institute for Research on Exceptional Children, University of Illinois. The current project is moving now into its final stages of data analysis and assessment of the findings.

THE PARENT PROJECT AND ITS PURPOSES

In order to show the place of the Category System in this research, I shall begin with a general description of what we have attempted to do and how we have gone about it. The work of this project represents the early descriptive and correlational phase of a long-term research program. The ultimate goal of this program is to develop a body of effective teaching procedures for cultivating the high-level thought processes and intellectual productivity of gifted children in the classroom.

We believe that the optimum development of the intellectual capacities and productivity of our more able or gifted children is a social and educational necessity. Research on the gifted [26] suggests that these children require a kind of intellectual stimulation and challenge beyond that provided by the general run of teaching methods and classroom practices now in use. The teacher who has bright or gifted children in her charge requires something beyond sound subject matter preparation. She

---

[1] The research reported here was supported jointly by the Cooperative Branch of the United States Office of Education and the University of Illinois (Project #965, U.S.O.E. Contract SAE-8969).

also needs training that will put her in command of the kinds of knowledge about gifted children and of such teaching procedures as will enable her to do this job effectively in the classroom.

Many teachers whose style is that of the lecturer teach in this way not out of preference, but perforce: they know no other way of handling the task. It is not always the case that these teachers take lecturing as the "easy way out." It is, rather, that they lack the skills and training necessary to stimulate active and thought-challenging discussion, and to sustain and direct its course into fruitful channels. To lead thinking without dominating it, to arouse students to a zestful pursuit of learning, is what some call the art of teaching [12]. The teacher who can do this sort of thing is often called "a born teacher," as if this ability were innate, one that could not be developed in ordinary mortals through training. But we believe this is not necessarily the case, though there may be more or less talented teachers. It seems more than likely that teachers in training, once given the opportunity to study the actual procedures and techniques of some of these rare "master" teachers—not by the usual brief in-class observation, but by careful analysis of these techniques *in process,* on class session tapescripts—then these master skills and techniques could be understood in detail and tried out by emulation in practice. One of the long-term goals of this research program is to develop effective means of training prospective teachers, to provide them with a repertoire of tactics and strategies that are basic to thought-stimulating instruction. Let teachers lecture out of preference, when lecturing is the sound strategy of the moment, and not because they do not know what else to do.

The task of the present research, then, is to provide some of the knowledge needed about gifted children, and about how their thinking shows up in classroom discussion, as a basis for later developmental and experimental phases of research. That is, we seek to learn from the present investigation what, it is hoped, will enable us eventually: (1) to develop a body of methods and procedures designed to tap and challenge high-level thought processes; (2) to test experimentally the relative effectiveness of these methods and procedures; and (3) to incorporate those which survive the test into improved training programs for classroom teachers—not only of the gifted, but eventually for teachers of all children who can profit from intellectually stimulating instruction.

Subjects and procedures. Approximately 260 children (chronological age from eleven through fourteen), in two junior high schools, constitute the subject population of this study. They represent the top 5 per cent of the general IQ population and were assigned to their classes on the basis of superior intellectual ability and past academic record.

We tested these children, then observed and tape-recorded their class sessions in English, social studies, and general science. The tests were used to secure data on the individual subject's self-concept, his attitudes toward school, peers, family, his future aspirations, etc.,[2] and data on such aspects of productive thinking as are taped in Guilford's batteries on ideational fluency, spontaneous flexibility, and sensitivity to problems [36]. Test data and observational data are being variously compared and correlated to determine the effects of a number of variables on the amount and kinds of productive thinking found in the classroom.

The subjects of this study were organized in five groups, each group representing two class sections of about twenty to twenty-five children each. The two sections per group were taped while under the instruction of a single teacher in a given subject-matter area. One of these groups has been tape-recorded in two subject-matter fields: General science and social studies. Each section was taped for at least five consecutive class sessions. Two observers took running notes, identifying speakers, and describing whatever nonspoken behaviors occurred during each session. All relevant materials (texts, charts, diagrams, board work, demonstration, apparatus, etc.) were noted and described so that this information could be included in the tapescript. Particular nuances of feeling tone, such as humor, reproach, puzzlement, etc., were also noted so that the "atmosphere" of the classroom might be preserved on the tapescript as much as possible. The teacher was requested to teach in her usual way, and to make no changes in her daily program or procedures during the taping sessions. We have found, incidentally, that after the first half hour or so, in most classes, both students and teachers seem to lose whatever self-consciousness they might have felt, and more or less forget our presence in the room. The tape recordings were then transcribed verbatim, audited for accuracy by the observers, and processed into transcripts for analysis.

DEVELOPMENT OF THE CATEGORY SYSTEM

The terminology of our Category System reflects its relationship to Guilford's conception of the *Structure of Intellect* [31]. After some preliminary consideration of other theoretical models of cognitive function—Piaget's conception of operational intelligence, for example—we decided that Guilford's model of the various dimensions of intelligence would best serve our purpose. For, although we are interested in the formal aspects of reasoning and conceptualization, we are also concerned with getting at the productive and the creative aspects of intellectual activity.

---

[2] These include a form of the Semantic Differential that has been used on a broader sample of children, and an adaptation of the Rhode-Hildreth Sentence Completion Test [49].

Guilford's three-dimensional model of intelligence. For years, educators and psychologists have expressed concern over the failure of conventional intelligence tests to tap the full range of human mental abilities. Such tests afford no measure of the individual's versatility and flexibility in problem solving, of the fluency and originality of his ideas, nor of his inventiveness; in other words, they make no measure of intellectual creativity. In World War II, the urgent need to identify individuals possessing such capacities stimulated research. J. P. Guilford, using factor-analytic techniques, tackled the problem. In working out a series of test batteries designed to tap these and other high-level abilities, Guilford formulated his model. A number of studies [28, 56] have since based their work on his three-dimensional model.

One dimension of Guilford's model consists in the *operations* of thinking, another in the *content* of the operations, and a third in the *products* of the operations within and upon the content. The operations consist in those activities of intelligence by means of which the organism deals with information. And "information" is defined in this theory as "that which the organism discriminates" [31]. There are four kinds of content: figural, symbolic, semantic, and behavioral. Figural content involves the perception of information possessing some degree of organization, as in a test for discovery of embedded figures, or in the comparison of geometric figures and forms. Symbolic content conveys information via mathematical symbols or musical notations, for example, or in the dials on the console of a computer. Semantic content has to do with meaning, with the messages conveyed in written or spoken language. It is this type of content which predominates in the classroom, even in classes dealing with mathematics and science subject matter. Behavioral content involves essentially nonverbal information and concerns "human interactions, where awareness of the attitudes, needs, desires, intentions, thought, etc., of other persons and of ourselves is important" [31]. Guilford and his associates have only recently undertaken to investigate this elusive social dimension of intelligence.

Although we are classifying instances of discussion behavior in terms of the thinking operations they reflect, we are also working out an analysis of these performances in terms of the products they may represent. We believe that such an analysis may render the written performances of our subjects—on their in-class written assignments testing productive thinking—more readily comparable to their oral performances in class discussion. It should also afford a useful basis for the analysis of textbook materials with respect to the kinds of thinking operations they require (or fail to require) of gifted students.

Productive thinking, as we conceive it, is thinking which the individual does "on his own." Not all such independent thinking, however, is necessarily, nor desirably, creative. Standardized tests of intelligence and school achievement provide a fairly adequate picture of the individual's capacity to think logically, to solve problems deductively. But in this study, we also needed some extraclass measure of the creative potential in the productive thinking of our subjects, in order to assess its possible correlates in classroom performance. Among a number of significant factors found to be associated with creative production are *ideational fluency,* i.e., having a rapid and varied flow of many ideas; *flexibility,* the ability to shift strategies readily in problem solving; *originality,* having ideas that are unusual, off-beat, unexpected, etc.; and *penetration,* or the ability to see beyond the simple and most obvious [36].

Accordingly, we gave two tests to our subjects. They have also been used by Getzels, and Jackson [28] and by Torrance and his associates [59, 56]. These are the Uses Test and the Consequences Test. Ideational fluency is measured in both tests simply in terms of the total number of responses given. Spontaneous flexibility is evidenced in the Uses Test by the *number* of different categories of use into which an item was placed, and in the Consequences Test by the varieties of implications proposed. Penetration is seen in the scope or conceptual breadth of responses in the Consequences Test; and originality is seen in the uniqueness or relative infrequency of a given response in terms of a test-measured, comparable population of some 650 subjects (including our present subjects).

In addition to the Uses and Consequences tests, we developed further measures of productive thinking in the form of in-class written assignments. These tests were designed to cover the subject-matter content dealt with in the class sections that we taped. They served also to provide written verbal fluency measures on students who did not talk up in class, or who were absent during all or part of the time we recorded their sessions. Rating scales and scoring manuals for these and the other tests administered to project subjects are currently in process of development and reliability assessment.

In adapting Guilford's model to the analysis of classroom verbal interaction, we have been obliged to make some modifications in his plan. Some of these are merely practical adjustments. Others represent extensions of his conception to account for kinds of cognitive behavior which simply would not occur in the situation of the individual "examinee" performing on one of Guilford's test batteries. The group interaction situation is quite a different one from that of the individual sitting by himself, left to his own resources, in responding to a test. We have found, however, that the over-all relevance and "fit" of the Structure of Intellect model to the context of group verbal interaction seem to be valid.

Types of verbal behaviors classified by the Category System. Four of the five primary categories of our System represent our use of Guilford's theory of thinking operations. These are *Cognitive-Memory* (C-M), *Convergent Thinking* (CT), *Divergent Thinking* (DT), and *Evaluative Thinking* (ET). The fifth primary category, *Routine* (R), encompasses the typical and familiar in-class give and take, along with various interpersonal maneuverings and other features of discussion behavior in which we are interested for present research purposes. (See the accompanying chart on page 60 which shows the organization of the symbols used in the System.)

Our Cognitive-Memory (C-M) category represents an assimilation of Guilford's operations of Cognition and Memory. This was done, since we are not concerned in this research to note such things as recognition, discovery, or perception, as such—at least, not as Guilford defines and identifies them in performances on his test batteries. Nor would it be feasible—even with a complete motion-picture and sound-track record of class proceedings—to identify such aspects of cognition with any degree of reliability. Accordingly, we assume cognition, and focus on those aspects of thinking operations which we describe in terms of their verbal correlates in classroom discourse.

As Cognitive-Memory (C-M) performances are defined, they involve no particular manipulation of ideas. We take them to represent only such thought processes as recognition, rote memory, and selective recall. Facts, ideas, and other remembered materials are *reproduced,* not produced in this primary category. We have broken Cognitive-Memory down into four secondary categories, each with its own symbol and subscript symbols. *Recapitulation* (Re), for example, involves such familiar classroom activities as quoting (Re_q), repetition (Re_p), recounting (Re_c), and review (Re_v). These are all verbal dealings with matters of immediate or recent past experience or discussion in class. Their names are more or less self-explanatory, and their symbols serve—as do all symbols in the Category System—as semantic cues for ready identification of the kinds of verbal performance they designate on the tapescripts. To give a bit more of the flavor of Cognitive-Memory, here are some examples. Fact-stating (Fs)[3] would be called for in this question: "Who was the sixteenth President of the United States?," and performed in the answer, "Abraham Lincoln."

[3] All locutions explicitly or conveniently requesting reply are represented by italicized symbols.

Organization of Aschner-Gallagher Category System*
(Gallagher-Aschner Project)

I. Routine (R)		II. Cognitive-Memory (C-M)		III. Convergent Thinking (CT)		IV. Evaluative Thinking (ET)		V. Divergent Thinking (DT)	
M	M_q	Scr		Tr		(U)	U_{ra}	(El)	s/f
	M_p						U_{ju}		
	M_a	(Re)	Re_q	(As)		(S)	S_{vp}	(Ad)	s/f
	M_{nc}		Re_p				S_{vc}		
	M_{fb}		Re_c	(Ex)	Ex_r			(Im)	s/f
	M_w		Re_v		Ex_v	(Q)	Q_j		
					Ex_n		Q_{-c}	(Syn)	
St	(St$_s$)	(Cl)	Cl_m	(Con)	Gen				
	St_o		Cl_q		Con_g				
	St_f				Con_l				
	St_c	(F)	F_s						
			F_d						
Ver	±1		F_m						
Verp	±1								
Agr	±1								
S									
Du									
Mu									
Hu									

* Circled items designate categories examined in Aschner-Wise "initiative" study.

Generally, the task set by a question is met and matched, whether ably or ineptly, by the reply. But this is not always the case. Here, for instance, is a question calling for review (Re_v): "What did we learn yesterday about the principles of Mercantilism?" The following kinds of answers might be given appropriately: "Would you say that again, please?" (Re_p), or "I was down at the principal's office when you covered that" (Re_o), or "Do you mean what we learned from Van Loon?," calling for Clarification of Meaning (*Clm*). Questions can "trigger" replies from the same or from different categories of performance. High-order thinking operations can be seen in replies to questions calling for no more than C-M operations, and vice versa. There is no inevitable bond between the kind of thinking "set" in the way a question is asked and the kind of thinking evinced in the reply. And this is one reason why the analyst must be extremely sensitive to the subtlest shifts and nuances of meaning conveyed in that context.

In Convergent Thinking (CT), we classify verbal behaviors taken to reflect thought processes that are both analytic and integrative, and that operate within a closely structured framework. Nevertheless, they are productive thought processes. Answers to questions and solutions to problems in the Convergent categories are reached by reasoning based on given and/or remembered data. Something more is involved than mere retrieval of remembered material; something is produced, though clearly not "invented" in any creative sense. We take this to be so whether or not the speaker, in dealing with a problem, gives explicit verbal evidence that he is using some rule, formula, or generalization. The archetype of Convergent Thinking is represented by the kind of reasoning that goes into the construction and "solution" of syllogisms, into our dealings with relationships in plane geometry, or in solving arithmetical problems. An oversimplified but apt example would be seen in such a question as: "If I had six apples and gave John two, how many apples would I have left?" The reply, "Four," would be classified as logical conclusion (Con_l) in our System.

A major Convergent category is that of Explanation (Ex). These performances deal variously with the conceptual ordering of ideas or phenomena in the substantiation or support of claims or conclusions about matters of fact, or about matters of value. Narrative explanation (Ex_n) may consist in an historical account of a sequence of events, as in describing the events that led to the Declaration of Independence; or it may involve a how-to-do-it type of procedural account. Rational explanation (Ex_r) involves the citation of material evidence, or rules to account for an event or to substantiate some claim or conclusion:

Ex_r
TEACHER: Why did the heavy weight slide down the plane faster than the light one? (Inclined on demonstration desk, made of rough surfaced board elevated at one end, propped up by two wooden blocks.)

Ex_r
STUDENT: Because the heavy weight overcame the resistance—the friction of the board's surface—better than the light one did. (NOTE: If this student's response had been in error, it would have still been classified as Ex_r, but tagged with a minus sign to indicate error.)

In a value explanation (Ex_v) reasons are offered in support or justification of some value-based claim, proposal, or conclusion:

Ex_v
TEACHER: Why do you say those men [Jamestown settlers] were irresponsible?

Ex_v
STUDENT: Well, they just stood around with their hands in their pockets and refused to work, even when they knew that winter was coming on.

Occasionally the question arises whether or not a given performance represents an instance of Convergent Thinking, or merely a recitation of something from memory. It is not always possible to answer this question for a given case, and when this happens, it seems best to classify on the minimum principle and assign the performance to a C-M category. But the immediate and past contexts of the class session often provide information enabling the analyst to decide. It must be determined, for example, whether or not the information called for in the question was handled earlier in discussion, or was treated in the current text and other course reading materials being covered by the class. The manner of the response itself sometimes provides a cue, as also does the phrasing of the question soliciting the response.

Evaluative Thinking (ET) includes three secondary categories. Each represents a type of framework within which value-based judgments are requested or expressed. In unstructured ET (U), the speaker is not restricted in his choice of criteria or in the range of his response along the dimension of judgment. Calling for and giving ratings exemplify this category:

U_{ra}
TEACHER: What do you think of MacArthur as a general?

U_{ra}
STUDENT: I think he was a pretty good military strategist.

U_{ra}
STUDENT: Well, I think he must have been an awful show-off, from some of the things I've read and heard about him.

Analysis of Verbal Interaction in the Classroom

In structured judgment (S), the speaker is presented with a limited scope within which to make an estimate (S_{vp}) or to state a choice (S_{vc}):

S_{vp}
TEACHER: When do you think we are likely to put a man safely on the surface of the moon?

S_{vp}
STUDENT: Well, from what I've picked up from reading about it—and what the experts are all saying—I'd guess we'll have a man up there in about five years.

S_{vc}
TEACHER: Which man was the stronger President, would you say, Adams or Jackson?

S_{vc}
STUDENT: I'd say Jackson.

Qualified judgments either side-step (Q_j) or expressly reject (Q_{-c}) choices made or called for.

Q_j
STUDENT: (responding to S_{vc} above) Well, that all depends on what you mean by "strong."

Q_{-c}
STUDENT: (in counter-judgment to S_{vc} above) Well, I'd say Adams was the stronger President, and *not* Jackson.

Another common problem of classification on tapescripts concerns overlap among categories. Tasks which engage thinking do not typically call for one kind of thinking operation, but for several. A question like "What sorts of things would you take to a desert island?" calls both Evaluative and Divergent Thinking into play. One way to approach this problem, in addition to consulting the context, is to distinguish between implicit and explicit requests for value judgments whenever possible. The cues often lie in the wording. In the "desert island" question above, the value dimension is implicit; hence the question would be classified as calling for divergent association (Ad_s). But if the question had been phrased: "Name three things you would most want to take to a desert island," then the value dimension is salient, and the divergent subordinate. The question—and the most likely reply—would thus receive a double classification—S_{vc}/Ad_s.

In Divergent Thinking (DT), we have developed four categories: *Elaboration* (El), *Divergent Association* (Ad), *Implications* (Im), and *Synthesis* (Syn). In these categories we have tried to "capture" features of verbal performance that are indicative of initiative, spontaneity, ideational fluency, originality and ingenuity, penetration and flexibility in problem solving, and the like.

Divergent Thinking seems to flourish or languish partly according to the conditions within which the individual operates, and partly as a function of the individual's own cognitive repertoire. We have arrived at a description of some of the conditions which invite or allow for divergent thinking: Problems and questions which invite divergent thinking provide for its operation within a definite framework, but one which is "data-poor" in such a way as to cast the person upon his own initiative and his own resources. There must be room and opportunity to generate many and varied ideas, associations, and conclusions.

Here are some examples of both free (f) and structured (s) divergent association (Ad):

Cl_m
TEACHER: (asking for clarification) You say there might be a population explosion over the continent?

Ad_f
STUDENT: Yes—well, I mean it would start at one spot and spread out from there—just like if a big bucket or container was suddenly dumped over and the water would spill out and spread out all over.

Ad_s
TEACHER: What comes to mind when you think of Plymouth Colony?

Ad_s
STUDENT: Well, there—to me it seemed like a time of suffering and hardship.

Ad_s
STUDENT: Well, the only thing I can think of is it seemed like every time you turned around, all of a sudden there was a war.

Implications (Im) involve the construction of "if-then" relationships. Consequences or antecedents are projected from given data to data not yet explicitly considered. The bearings or implications of given ideas, situations, events, actions, etc. upon affairs not yet specified are sought, "seen," or postulated. These performances represent the counterpart in discussion of those elicited on the Consequences tests. Here are some examples:

Im_s
TEACHER: Suppose Spain had not been defeated when the Armada was destroyed in 1588. Suppose instead that Spain had conquered England. What would the world be like today if that had happened?

Im_s
STUDENT: Well, we might all be speaking Spanish over here.

Im_s
STUDENT: We might have fought a Revolutionary War with Spain instead of England.

Analysis of Verbal Interaction in the Classroom

Im_s
STUDENT: Maybe Spain would have had a world empire like England had—with the sun never setting on it.

Im_t
STUDENT: (in the context of current events discussion) If we get one of our astronauts on the moon ahead of Russia, maybe old Khrushchev would lose face with the Russian people.

Synthesis (Syn) classifies what we consider to be a high-order divergent performance. It is invariably spontaneous. On his own initiative, the individual "takes off" from the central idea under discussion and proceeds to transform it or integrate it into some entirely new point or frame of reference. It is an unexpected, though generally relevant, tie-in with current discussion; sometimes it consists in a reversal or variation on the central theme being discussed. Synthesis may be relatively simple, or represent highly complex integrations of many ideas. It is a type of performance which may be provided for but not directly solicited by the posing of questions or problems. Here are a few examples of Synthesis:

Ad_s
TEACHER: How many different ways can you get 12?

Ad_s
STUDENT: 4 + 8; 6 + 6; 16 − 4; 48 ÷ 4, etc., etc.

Syn
STUDENT: You can count to 9 in the base 10 number system and that'll give you 12 in the base 6 number system.

Syn
STUDENT: (context: Fifteenth-Century Age of Exploration) It looks like we're moving into another Age of Exploration today, only this time it'll be new worlds instead of New World!

Syn
STUDENT: (context: School Segregation and Civil Rights) I can see this whole question of civil rights coming up again when we start colonizing other planets.

Synthesis seems to represent a form of intellectual play with ideas. But it also represents a mode of thinking which can be highly creative. For it is often out of the experimental, seemingly playful juxtaposition of ideas that insights and discoveries of great consequence are born.

Routine (R) is a primary category into which we classify types of performance viewed, not from the standpoint of the thinking operations they may involve, but for their bearing on the thinking that goes on in class discussion. Routine includes performances that are both verbal and nonverbal; they represent the typical aspects of the day-to-day direction, conduct, and/or personal reaction to what is said and done in class. Management (M), for example, has to do with the mechanics of the class session, involving the typical announcements, roll-calling, permission-giving, assignment-making, and direction-giving activities by means of which the procedures of the group are carried on. Typical of this category are such remarks as: "Open your textbooks to page 79," or "The basketball game scheduled for tonight has been cancelled," or "Miss Jones, may I ask a question?" etc.

Structuring (St) is a more interesting type of behavior. It represents a conventional engineering move which, in discussion, serves to shape or frame in advance the content and conduct of subsequent class activity. Self-structuring (St_s) represents a fairly sophisticated form of verbal maneuver. It consists in a prefatory or preliminary move by means of which the speaker indicates what he is about to say and, often, the standpoint from which he wishes his next remarks to be taken. Here are some examples of self-structuring:

St_s
STUDENT: Well, I have two points to make. First of all, it is . . . , and secondly, it would be necessary to . . . , etc.

St_s
STUDENT: Well, going back to what Bill said, I think . . . , etc.

St_s
STUDENT: This is kinda off the point, but . . . , etc.

St_s
STUDENT: Well, there are at least three reasons why that could have happened. First . . . , etc.

St_s
STUDENT: Now I am not quite sure this is right, but . . . , etc.

The speakers in the examples above are gifted boys and girls in grade seven-eight (called subfreshman at their school).

Verdict (Ver) is another important type of behavior we keep track of on the tapescripts, along with Humor (Hu), Agreement (Agr), Self-reference (S), Dunno (Du), and Muddled (Mu). All these categories reflect variously the social-psychological tenor of the class session, as they show up in individual performances. Verdict is a pronouncement on deportment and/or on the quality of an academic performance. It expresses either praise (+) or reproach (—), and is more often directed toward an individual than toward the group, more often rendered by teachers than by students. We distinguish between the more typical impersonal verdicts that teachers give when they are pleased or displeased with a student's performance and the less common personal form which Verdict sometimes takes. To convey the emotional tone differences implied in this contrast, here are some examples:

+Ver
TEACHER: Now that's a good point. (or) That's an interesting point, Sam. (or) I'm glad to see so many hands up on that question.

—Ver
TEACHER: Well, that's not a very pertinent idea to bring in at this point, Tim. (or) I think you'll find the facts to be otherwise, Tom. (or) I'm afraid that's not quite right.

+Verp
TEACHER: You did a fine job, Mary, I'm pleased with you. (or) Class, you've really made me happy with the job you did on the test. (or) Well, I know someone who did *her* homework.

—Verp
TEACHER: Now cut that out! (or) Harry, you put that pencil down and sit still! (or) Well, if you'd read your assignment you'd *have* an answer!

—Verp
STUDENT: (implied personally but not explicitly expressed) I don't see the point of all this. (or) Why don't we get something done in this class for a change? (or) I don't see why we have to write such long papers. (or) Aw, gee whiz—that's too much!

In keeping track of Verdict, we are looking for possible connections between the frequency and manner in which verdicts are given in a classroom and the subsequent performances of the individual students who receive them, and between teacher verdicts and the general level of subsequent performance in the class as a whole.

Procedures used in classifying protocol materials. After duplication, tapescripts are prepared for later coding and tabulation. Each successive speaker's performance is broken down into its constituent "thought units."[4] A single utterance may consist of one or a series of these units. Breaks between units are indicated by slash marks on the tapescript. Breaks are made on the basis of a distinct shift in the speaker's performance from one category or subcategory to another. Overly fine distinctions are avoided in order to include in one unit whatever can be taken as representing no marked shift into another category.

Four trained analysts, working independently, then code each tape-

[4] These "thought" units are not to be confused with the episode and monologue units [7, 8] that are used to mark off serial instances of speaker-speaker(s) interaction, or speaker "solo" performance. The Aschner-Gallagher units fall *within* individual performances, which may then be later incorporated into the broader "group interaction" units. In this project, we intend to use episode and monologue units to trace patterns of teacher-student interaction sequences, in terms of Aschner-Gallagher thought units, as coded beforehand.

script. Independent codings are thereafter compared. Disagreements are discussed, and category status is decided by group consensus. Disagreements occur rarely at the primary category level. The percentage of interjudge agreements per unit, at the subcategory level, approximates .69 to .79 on the average. We believe that, in its present form, the Category System has achieved a satisfactory and workable level of reliability. Of course, it is assumed that further improvements will be made on the System as we go along. We do not expect, however, that this or any other coding instrument of this kind could ever achieve 100 per cent reliability.

Symbols from coded tapescripts are then transferred to flow charts, so that recurrent patterns of thought production in teacher-student and student-student interaction sequences may be more readily traced. Summary tabulations of coded thought units, and of group interaction units, are made from these flow charts, both for particular individuals and for entire class groups.

Some observations and comments. We have found that the classroom situation both releases and restricts thinking activities in ways that are quite different from the test situation. We are more likely to see spontaneity and the self-triggered shifting of the speaker's performance from one primary category of operation to another than we are to see it on one of Guilford's tests. In most classes we have studied so far, boys do more talking than girls do. Yet, on in-class written work, girls are often more fluent—and definitely more articulate—than boys. In respect to Divergent Thinking, we may see a lot of rather fluffy inconsequential responses in this category, "off the top of the head." That is, they reveal no very great or high quality in this kind of thinking just because it is divergent.

In this connection, by the way, it should not be assumed that we are more interested in Divergent Thinking than in any other kind of thinking, nor that we want more Divergent Thinking than any other kind of thinking to go on in the classroom. It is true that we esteem the creativity and inventiveness that divergent questions call for, and that occasionally come forth spontaneously in the classroom. We are glad to see a classroom situation open enough to foster free play of imagination. We do think, however, that the consistently low frequencies at which Divergent Thinking has been found to occur so far on our tapescripts are too limited. Nevertheless, we are not faddists; we are not bedazzled by the notion of creativity. We hope most of all to discover some basis for striking a good educational balance among the various categories of thinking. And by such a balance, we mean one that is not only most likely to foster all types of thinking operations, but one that is pedagogically sound, in terms of the subject matter at hand and the type (or types) of learning tasks which this content may involve.

It should also be made clear that we do *not* value class discussion as *the one* best use of classroom time, no matter how intellectually stimulating such discussion may be. Nor do we assume that silences and pauses during discussion represent spates of "no thinking." In the current research, we are concerned with relating student performances during class discussion to a number of intraclass and extraclass variables. But as educators, we are concerned that class discussion—when and as it is carried on—fulfill its proper function as the occasion for optimum stimulation and development of the higher-level thinking processes, and of the learning that issues in and from their operation.

Scope and limits on use of Category System of this design. As indicated, we now feel reasonably satisfied with the stability and reliability of the Category System. The categories it contains seem to cover most, if not all, of the different kinds of cases that we encounter; no new categories need be created to handle "problem cases." Of course, problem cases still come up, and they always will. But this is due to the fact that it is not always possible to know exactly what someone is saying or doing with the words he speaks—not even if one is in his presence as he speaks. Language has its built-in and inevitable ambiguities.

Although all the categories defined in the System do appear on some tapescripts, some of them occur rarely in general, or even fail to occur at all on many tapescripts. This is related more to differences from class to class, and to the ways teachers run their classes, than to the nature of the Category System itself. On the other hand, it can be seen—especially among the subcategories at the secondary level—that further distinctions or different distinctions could have been made. This relates to the limitations that we deliberately imposed on the scope of the System in the interests of economy of analysts' time and efficiency. The more categories in the System, the more fine discriminations and codings will be made. We drew the line where we did in the reasonable hope that the System covered all the varieties of behaviors that we should need in pursuing the goals of the present research.

SOME PRELIMINARY APPLICATIONS OF THE SYSTEM IN THE PARENT PROJECT

The proportionate frequencies of verbal production found on tapescripts, among the five primary categories of the System, are not difficult to anticipate. On the whole, Routine and Cognitive-Memory occur most often on most tapescripts. Next comes Convergent Thinking, then Evaluative Thinking, and finally, least often, Divergent Thinking.

The general performance of a science class, taped on this project, in relation to other class sessions tabulated so far, is considerably above average in frequency of Convergent performance, above in Divergent, and about average in the Evaluative Thinking category. The Routine category is about average in proportionate frequency to the rest of what goes on in a class session, while there is somewhat lower relative frequency of Cognitive-Memory performances. Whether this is mainly a function of the instruction techniques, of the course subject matter, or of the particular phase at which the class is operating in the treatment of the topic at hand, is not determinable from these tabulations of one class session. But a total picture of all science class sessions, when compared variously with tapescripts from classes in other subject areas—including those of this class—should provide some indication of what factors seem to be most influential in determining the amount and quality of thinking that occurs in the junior high school science classes we have taped.

One goal of this study is to check on the stability or fluctuations in the individual child's performance from one class session to the next, from one teacher to another, from one subject matter to another. In addition, of course, the child's IQ and personality, and also his home background data, are examined in relation to his classroom performance in efforts to determine what factors seem to have a bearing on its characteristic quality.

A preliminary exploration of sex differences in thought production has been carried out recently in one of the project's social studies classes. Gallagher calls attention to the fact that in this class, "the boys seemed to be consistently more fluent verbally, and in the flow of ideas in all expressive areas" [27]. The relative proportions, however, among the different thought areas were quite similar in boys and girls. Whether these findings will be paralleled in other class groups and with other teachers remains to be seen in the further analyses and comparisons to be made.

AN EXPLORATION OF STUDENT INITIATIVE IN CLASS DISCUSSION[5]

Let me turn now to a little study that Mr. Arthur Wise and I are just getting under way. We are examining student classroom discussion behaviors in terms of the amount and kinds of intellectual initiative displayed by students in relation to a number of variables.

---

[5] The study reported here was financed by a Public Health Service Research Grant (#MH 05120–02) from the National Institutes of Health, United States Public Health Service, to Harvard Universtiy for the Center for Cognitive Studies.

Analysis of Verbal Interaction in the Classroom

The term "initiative" has a favorable connotation in our hurly-burly, busy society. People who get things done, who do things without being pushed or prodded into doing them, are said to have initiative. And when "initiative" appears in letters of recommendation, job candidates so labeled will be favorably considered for many kinds of business and professional positions. Is initiative related in any way to intelligence, we wonder? How about initiative and intellectual creativity—inventiveness, ingenuity, imagination? Are there sex differences in initiative? If so, are they related to other variables than intelligence and creativity? If initiative is prized in our society, how does it fare in the classroom? What classroom conditions foster or inhibit its occurrence, its development? These are some of the questions that we have set out to investigate.

"INITIATIVE" DEFINED FOR THIS STUDY

In the present study—one of a series planned in an investigation of "student style" in the classroom—we have chosen to define "initiative" in terms of its intellectual dimensions rather than in its broader sense, as denoting any and all kinds of behavior of the "self-starter" variety. For this reason, in applying the Aschner-Gallagher Category System to the set of tapescripts to be examined, we ruled out certain categories of performance and included others. (See Organization of Symbols of Aschner-Gallagher System.)

We ruled out all instances of students' unsolicited procedural questions or comments, and all those involving the relatively trivial cognitive behaviors represented by Scribe (Scr) and Translation (Tr). We also excluded, for the present, all interpersonal maneuvering categories, save Self-structuring (St_s). This is a form of student behavior that is invariably self-initiated, and about which we have a hypothesis that I shall discuss shortly. We included all categories of student performance that are taken to exhibit thinking operations on semantic content, but we classified only those instances explicitly dealing with the course content or subject matter of the class. We did not classify teacher performances except in cases where the teacher's performance either directly solicited initiative, or at least permitted its occurrence.

Accordingly, we classify instances of student initiative on the tapescripts in the following forms:

1. *Completely unsolicited* (not necessarily unwelcome) *and "spontaneous" performances.* These are most clearly typified in Synthesis (Syn) and Self-structuring (St_s), as these were described earlier.

2. *Responses that "go beyond the call of duty" in their ways of dealing with the task at hand.* Suppose, for example, a student is asked to give reasons why X is the case (Ex_r). He does so, and in the doing, he

may illustrate or elaborate his point by offering parallel cases or examples (El_t); or he may construct an appropriate simile or analogy (Ad_t); or he may go on to predict something further about X (Im_t).

3. *Responses offered in contexts where initiative is invited but not required.* These are typically found following questions designed either to open up or wind up discussion. For example, a teacher may open discussion with this sort of question: "Would any of you like to ask questions or make some comments on the [assigned] story you read last night?" And teachers often bring discussion to its closing phase with such questions as: "Any questions or comments on this, before we go on?" or, "Anybody want to have his say on this, or raise some further questions?" These "Open Questions," as we call them (OQ), typically give rise to self-initiated responses in any or all of the primary categories. Children may ask procedural questions (R), factual questions (C-M), or venture or request judgments or opinions (ET); they may call for or volunteer explanations (CT); or they may come forth with some form of divergent question or comment (DT). In responses to this type of question, "anything goes." However, Open Questions do not seem to trigger off any great proportion of high-level thinking, even in classes of gifted children.

4. *Responses addressed to questions demanding initiative.* Such responses follow on questions calling for Divergent Thinking. Here the student may not volunteer a reply, and unless the teacher "tags" him —calls on him when his hand was not raised—he is not required to speak. But if the student responds to such a question—for example, to, "How many ways can you think of to attract more tourists from Europe to visit our country?"—then he is put on his own initiative by the very nature of the question. He may come up with something he heard or read about, of course, but it is his own choosing and thinking in proposing this idea to this question at this time. Naturally, there is a range of quality in responses to such initiative-tapping questions. Some children echo with variants of earlier responses of their classmates to the current question. And as the number of responses following a divergent question increases, there is a marked drop in the quality of some responses and an equally striking rise in "way-out," almost far-fetched responses.

Subjects and procedures. In the original outline of this paper, I planned to take up the notion of "Structure-Context" at this point. But now it seems much more appropriate to lay the groundwork for that part of the discussion by giving you some concrete information about the subjects of our study, and what we are looking for at this stage of the investigation.

We are currently exploring relationships between intelligence and initiative both within and across class groups. We have also made some preliminary examinations of sex differences. We have IQ data on students in only seven classes on tapescripts; these data are comparable in subject matter areas—English, social studies, and English–social studies—and could also provide us with a wide range of intelligence levels and various types of ability grouping. The enormous fund of data that might be drawn from the Smith project tapes is not generally accessible to us, since IQ data on those classes were not available except in two high schools. The names of student speakers were not always noted on the Smith tapes, nor were any records on the numbers of students enrolled, or the number of students present or absent during a given class session. This is unfortunate but, after all, it was not necessary for the purposes of the Smith project to have these data. However, we have managed to include four schools, to cover comparable subject matters in class discussions from grades seven through twelve, and to include IQ's from as low as 58 (Binet) to 185 (CTMM), with a population of 156 subjects—seventy girls and eighty-six boys. The subjects range in chronological age from twelve through seventeen.

Three of the four schools are located in rather prosperous suburban communities in the Chicago metropolitan area; the fourth (in a central Illinois university town) is a laboratory school for gifted children, admitting them for a five-year junior and senior high school period on completion of the sixth grade. Two of our seven class groups were tape-recorded in this laboratory school.[6] The one educable mentally handicapped (EMH) class (mean Binet IQ, 69) we have was under instruction in a suburban high school. These students were operating at about the fourth-grade level in reading and arithmetic. A third group of gifted students—all in U.S. history, grade twelve (mean IQ 129)—and two heterogeneously grouped classes were taped in a second suburban high school. One of the latter, a "core" English–social studies class, grade nine, ranges in IQ from 101 to 144—with a mean of 117—while the other, in eleventh-grade English, ranged in IQ from 73 to 125, with a mean of 106. The three classes in this school had been measured on the Henmon-Nelson group test. A third heterogenous group, in U.S. history, grade eleven, was tested in their school on the Terman McNemar group test. The IQ range in this class runs from 86 to 138, with a mean score of 114.

We have not, at this stage, run any cross-group correlations of IQ and initiative, since the seven groups are not comparable on IQ, though

[6] One of these "subfreshman" classes, as they are called, when tested on the CTMM, had a mean score of 138; the other group was given the Lorge-Thorndike, showing a mean score of 129.

we plan to do so, by conversion to standard scores. We also plan to run internal analyses, using the Pearson r formula for tracing whatever linear correlation may show up between IQ and initiative, and probably a biserial or a rank correlation between sex and initiative. But since these are all relatively small groups, the resulting correlations will hardly test our hypotheses.

Our general hypotheses have already been stated, in question form, on page 71 of this paper. We are currently exploring four subsidiary hypotheses concerning relationships between IQ and particular kinds of initiative:

1. *Self-structuring* (St_s) will be positively related to high IQ. That is, the higher the IQ's, and the greater the number of high IQ's within a class group, the greater will be the frequency of St_s responses.

2. *Synthesis* (Syn) will hold relatively the same high frequencies in relation to high IQ's, as St_s above.

3. *Complex responses*—those containing at least three Aschner-Gallagher units, of which at least one is self-initiated—will occur more frequently as IQ's increase in "height" and "density" in a class group.

4. *Extended-complex responses*—those containing more than three Aschner-Gallagher units, and which involve two or more self-initiated units—will occur more frequently as IQ ranges go higher, and as high IQ's increase in number in a given group.

In this exploratory study, we used only two complete tapescripts per class group, or fourteen tapescripts in all. In all cases we chose class sessions that followed at least one hour of prior tape-recording—to rule out the "mike-fright" diffidence that might possibly show up on the first day's taping of a class. Mr. Wise, who had no part in the development of the Category System, underwent one full-time week—about forty hours—of intensive training in coding tapescripts by application of the System. We used "practice" tapescripts, none representing any of the seven classes included in this study. Then we took duplicate scripts and went our separate ways. We compared and cross-checked each other's codings. Because there were only two of us, it was important to avoid ready agreement—on his side or mine when problem cases arose. Accordingly, we really thrashed out our differences, and when we finally reached agreement, it was agreement that held up over time. That is, after two or three weeks, in rechecking old "problem cases" on a given tapescript, we almost never found it necessary to reopen the question as to the code-status of the cases. Further confirmation of our "reliability" has come from Gallagher Project findings now coming in; they agree with ours—or perhaps I should say, we agree with theirs.

THE STRUCTURE-CONTEXT OF DISCUSSION

Before reporting our initial findings, it would be appropriate here to indicate what we mean by "Structure-Context." As we searched the tapescripts, looking for initiative, it became evident beyond all question that the way the teacher handles the discussion situation is the one most influential factor in determining the presence or the total absence of student initiative in class discussion. In an eleventh-grade class in U.S. history, we have a classic example of a situation in which initiative is all but ruled out. This teacher lectures, punctuating each packaged paragraph of discourse with a question to which "the answer" is a fact reported in the history books. One student recites the fact called for, and the teacher moves on to another paragraph of discourse. In this tapescript, representing one 55-minute class session, only three cases of student initiative occur. In one case, a girl asks the teacher a fact question in response to the teacher's fact question—perhaps in an effort to understand the question she was expected to answer. The other two cases occurred as follows:

TEACHER: Are there any questions you'd like to ask—things that I might have suggested to you—at this time? Steve?

STEVE: Well, only on that voting there. What is the Christian state—I mean, Christian province?

TEACHER: Any more questions? Mary Jane?

MARY JANE: Well, does the United States still have any connections in the Philippines? Because I don't think us kids know much about it.

These were the only initiative-soliciting questions asked on the entire tapescript. Moreover, no further student questions of any kind were addressed to either of the two Open Questions. In each case the teacher launched into a long monologue—one running over six hundred words in length. Then the bell rang. This teacher's style did not vary from the pattern described and illustrated above throughout the five class sessions taped! That was how one week of social studies went by in the life of this class.

Another Structure-Context typical of many class discussions is seen when a student chairman "runs" the discussion, with the teacher coaching or moving in *ad libitum* from the side lines. In these situations, there is much more student initiative, on the whole, than when the teacher is conducting the proceedings. But there is often a kind of "pre-cooked" or programmed character in the student chairman's questions. This type of situation seems at best to reach the Open Question level of initiative solicitation, with several speakers responding before the chairman shifts discussion to the "next question on the list." Students seem to feel freer to speak up to a classmate in the role of chairman than they do when the teacher invites open discussion. But in the long run, it is the types of teacher-set questions which the chairman transmits that determine how much leeway class members will have, regarding the kinds of intellectual initiative they may or will take. Incidentally, we do not classify the performances of student chairmen for initiative, since their role is predefined as initiating and "leading" discussion. Moreover, the way in which the teacher operates "from the side lines" may either serve to quell or to stimulate initiative in the group. Again, it all depends on the kinds of questions the teacher asks, or the ways in which he or she engineers student participation in the discussion.

Tightly structured questions may either totally preclude initiative, as in the history class mentioned above, or they may demand and stimulate initiative, as observed in another teacher's class.

As a result of these observations, we decided to discriminate three levels or types of Structure-Contexts in which cases of initiative would be tabulated, as they occurred:

1. *Spontaneous.* Here we counted all completely unsolicited cases—such as Synthesis, Self-structuring, all DT responses of the free (f) variety, along with such items as judgments and opinions (ET) offered or called for, and cases of convergent thinking (CT). We counted students' unsolicited fact questions also at this level, despite their low-order cognitive status, if they were "on the subject" (nonprocedural), and if they represented genuine cases of unsolicited initiative.

2. *Open Question.* Here we tabulated all cases—according to whatever categories they represented—of responses to questions or other devices by which discussion is invited, or "thrown open to the group."

3. *Structured.* This is the "tight" level of performance at which no initiative may be invited by the question, but which does not necessarily bar its occurrence. Here also we count the initiative-demanding questions that leave the student no choice but to take some degree of initiative if he addresses his reply to the question.

Each coded response was tabulated at the particular Structure-Context level at which it occurred. This gave us a rough picture of the over-all patterns and shifts in Structure-Contexts, both within individual class groups and across groups. There are obviously many ways in which individual and group responses may be studied in relation to their Structure-Context types or levels.

PRELIMINARY FINDINGS

We have summarized the results of the first analyses we have made of our data, relating IQ to initiative *within* four class groups, using tapescripts that cover two 56-minute class sessions per group. In these, IQ's were broken down into three levels, although the lowest of the low—in either gifted group—represents a score in the top 5 per cent of the general IQ population.

One group very nicely confirms our hypotheses about the positive relationship between IQ and amount and kinds of initiative the students displayed in discussion. Both were "gabby groups," clearly, as seen in their respective gross totals of initiative-coded thought units. The high frequency of Self-structuring (St_s) and of Extended-complex responses is also noteworthy. In none of the other five classes, nor in any of the many other classes studied thus far, has there been anything even approximating these frequencies.

A second group would have offered another small confirmation of our hypotheses, but for one case, a boy we identify here as Ste, who falls in the low IQ group ($n=7$) in his class. Take Ste out, however, and everything goes nicely as before. There is no explaining Ste on the data currently examined. But it is striking that in gross total units of initiative, Ste racked up 44 out of the 101 coming from the "Lo" group, and nearly 25 per cent of the total production of the entire class group! With respect to Structure-Context, both of these gifted groups were invited or required often to take the initiative in thinking. Both teachers operate in a similar response-stimulating style.

At this point we are only enticed further by these results. But they merely offer trail-markers on the road to generalization. We have surely, still, a long way to go.

The U.S. history class, grade eleven, is a widely heterogeneous group in terms of IQ range (Terman-McNemar 83–138). Here again, but for one boy, Jac, in the medium IQ group ($n=9$) of his class, the hypotheses seem to hold. However, one might wonder if the relatively low gross total of initiative units (59) in this group is a function of the personalities and abilities of the class members, or is it perhaps related more to the fact that this is one of those groups which operates with a student chairman, and quite consistently at the OQ Structure-Context level? So far as types of initiative go, however, even counting Jac, there is a very slight trend in favor of the high IQ's—except with respect to St_s, where the low IQ's ($n=8$) outdid the high IQ's ($n=8$)! What these few results will signify later, when we have more data on comparable groups, remains uncertain.

The EMH group seems to bear out our hunches on how IQ relates to certain kinds of student initiative. But it is worth noting that these thirteen youngsters produced a gross total of 71 initiative units, as compared with the total of 59 units produced by the twenty-five-member class of "high average" IQ juniors just discussed. Is the teacher-determined

Structure-Context at work here? This specially trained teacher of the educable mentally handicapped maintained an easy, informal, open, and often humorous give and take with the class. Students were free to speak up spontaneously, and they did so—often.

As you can see, these preliminary findings are typical—they raise more questions than they answer. But Mr. Wise and I believe we may be on the trail of something well worth tracking down.

THE SCIENTIFIC STUDY OF TEACHER BEHAVIOR

DONALD M. MEDLEY
*Division of Teacher Education
The City University of New York*
AND
HAROLD E. MITZEL
The Pennsylvania State University

THE RESEARCH WE HAVE BEEN DOING IN THE DIVISION OF TEACHER EDUcation of The City University of New York comes from the tradition of educational rather than psychological research. We decided to study classroom behavior not in order to test or develop any theory of behavior (although we may yet come to that), but in order to find out what the graduates of our teacher education program were doing in their classrooms. We wanted to find out what patterns of classroom behavior were characteristic of those graduates who were effective teachers, in the fond hope of relating effective behaviors of graduates to something in the training we had given them.

In attacking this problem, we have made use of at least five assumptions (that we are aware of). We have assumed, first of all, that *the most promising approach is a quantitative approach.* To us it seems obvious that the modern method of science is quantitative in nature. The tremendous contributions to knowledge made by the physical sciences seem to us to be the direct result of the success physicists have had in quantifying the aspects of physical phenomena relevant to their problems. Newton's laws of motion could neither have been formulated nor verified without the mass of measurement data in the areas of mechanics and astronomy which were available to him; nor could Einstein's theory have been formulated on the basis of the data available to Newton; his more inclusive theory had to wait on improvements in instrumentation and the amassing of quantitative data utilizing those improvements. It is our contention that no general theory of classroom behavior can be formulated until ways of quantifying classroom behaviors have been developed, and a large body of measurements of behaviors using these methods has been assembled. The fact that the phenomena we study are vastly more complex than the phenomena of physics makes the employment of the quantitative method all the more necessary.

We have also assumed that in order to learn anything about classroom behavior *it is necessary to study behavior in the classroom:* we have *not* assumed (as many psychologists seem to assume) that it is possible to learn something about classroom behavior by studying laboratory behavior; or that much can be found out about how pupils learn by studying how college students, apes, or white mice learn. We have not found it necessary to assume the existence of laws of learning which are uniform across subjects, learning tasks, learning environments, and species. We have eschewed research, the findings of which are applicable to the classroom only through analogy.

We have tried to avoid any use of analogous reasoning except, perhaps, in the generation of hypotheses to be tested. We take the position that a conclusion drawn from a specific study may be applied only to other teachers, pupils, or classes which could be drawn at random from a population of teachers, pupils, or classes which could also contain the teachers, pupils, or classes studied. While it is not always easy to decide whether two subjects could come from the same population, it is sometimes easy to tell when two subjects could *not*. It seems obvious, for example, that a pupil and a mouse, or a psychological laboratory and a third-grade classroom, or a tachistoscope and a kindergarten teacher, could not both be simple random samples from single populations of pupils, classrooms, or teachers—or of mice, laboratories, or tachistoscopes, for that matter.

A third basic assumption we have made is that any effect the teacher has on the pupils is mediated by some overt behavior on the teacher's part. If the behavior takes place in the classroom, *it is therefore capable of being seen or heard by a properly trained observer*. If this assumption is not tenable, then the task of studying teachers' classroom behavior by the objective scientific method must be regarded as impossible.

We further assume that *each behavior a teacher exhibits has a purpose* (conscious or unconscious), and may be effective in achieving that purpose to a greater or less degree. The competence of a teacher is defined as the average success of all of his behaviors in achieving their intended effects. Strictly speaking, we cannot assess the competence of a particular teacher unless we know what effects he is seeking to achieve. We can, however, measure certain effects of his behavior and see which of his behaviors are followed by effects in which we are interested. If this information were made known to the teacher, he could presumably modify his behavior and increase his competence. There are as many ways of being effective as there are effects to be produced; the competent teacher is able to select those modes of behavior which will produce the effects he intends to produce. As research workers, we have studied effectiveness, rather than competence. Let someone else wrestle with the problem of teacher competence, since it involves value judgments which we do not regard as part of the province of science.

Our fourth assumption is that *what the teacher does is an important factor in determining what the pupil learns.* We do not rule out the pupil's capacity, maturation, or school and neighborhood environment as important factors; we hold that teacher behavior is also important, and have chosen to study it.

Finally, I suppose we have also assumed that, once effective patterns of teacher behavior have been identified, it will be possible to teach education students how to exhibit them. At least we have hoped that this is true. If, as some investigators seem to believe, teacher behaviors are manifestations of teacher personality characteristics not likely to be affected by college courses, then the problem of staffing the schools is a selection problem rather than a training problem. We choose to assume that teachers could learn to behave more effectively without undergoing any basic personality change, if only we knew enough about effective behavior to teach them how.

The development of a science of effective teacher behavior is almost certainly the most urgent research problem that faces the profession today. If teaching is not a science, then it must be an art—that is, a skill possessed only by teachers who either were born that way, or have been lucky enough to stumble on its secrets by chance. Without definite knowledge of the nature of effective teaching, it is impossible either to identify and recruit those young people born with this talent, or to make successful teachers out of young people born without it.

To form an estimate of the present state of the science of teacher behavior, it is only necessary to perform the following simple experiment: Think of the one principle or rule of teaching behavior which to you seems least open to question—the one which you would pass on to a beginning teacher with the greatest certainty that it would be useful to him. Then consider the nature of the evidence on which that principle is based.

Is it based on a series of carefully controlled research studies which have demonstrated its validity beyond reasonable doubt? Or is the principle accepted because it agrees with modern educational philosophy? Or does the evidence rest on successful personal experiences of teachers who believe in the principle and try to follow it?

The fact is that very few of the things teachers do in classrooms today are done because they have been demonstrated scientifically to be effective ways of behaving. An honest appraisal of the content of teacher training would reveal that it does not resemble the rigorous quantitative set of laws which form the substance of the training of architects or engineers as much as it resembles the treasured store of traditions passed on by one witch doctor to another. No doubt the principles followed by teachers have more validity than those followed by the witch doctor, but both are based on the same kind of evidence. Indeed, many educators openly express the conviction that teaching is a mysterious, almost magical process which nobody understands or can hope to understand thoroughly. Possibly much of this lore is perfectly true—we are not yet in a position to advocate that any of it be thrown out. But progress comparable to that seen in the physical sciences can only be achieved when teaching becomes a science.

Scientifically based knowledge of the nature of effective teacher behavior must be sought in studies attempting to relate teacher behavior to teacher effectiveness; if the quantitative scientific method is to be used, each such study must obviously incorporate objective measurements of both types of variables. Domas and Tiedeman [20] have listed over a thousand investigations related to teacher competence; although many of them do not attempt to relate behavior and effectiveness, there are a number of studies which do. Why have these studies contributed so little to the science of effective behavior?

Aside from the fact that practically nobody reads these old studies any more, there are two cogent reasons why their impact has been so slight. First of all, the vast majority of the research in teacher effectiveness that has been done must be discarded as irrelevant because the criteria of effectiveness used have been invalid. Second, an even larger part of the research must be rejected because it has failed to incorporate any objective measures of teacher behavior. Mitzel and Gross [44], in a critical review of attempts to measure teacher effectiveness, found only about twenty studies which used measures which met their criteria; Medley and Mitzel [41], in a similar review of studies of teacher behavior, also found only some twenty studies which incorporated objective measures of behavior. There is not much overlap between the two lists, so it seems safe to say that the serious student of the science of effective teacher behavior would need to consult only about forty research reports among the hundreds that have been done to have read all of those which are germane to his purpose.

The question of why so much of the research in teacher effectiveness has not led to usable results will be discussed in terms of two problems: the problem of measuring teacher effectiveness and the problem of measuring teacher behavior.

THE PROBLEM OF MEASURING TEACHER EFFECTIVENESS

It is widely agreed [see, for example, 13, 1, 46] that the ultimate criterion of teacher effectiveness must be based on changes in pupils. Intermediate criteria must be shown to be relevant, that is, correlated with the ultimate criterion. There are many factors which make it difficult to measure a teacher's effectiveness in producing changes in pupil behaviors. Some of the difficulties are philosophical or definitional in nature and relate to the selection of which changes are to be measured. These problems call for a willingness on the part of the research worker to take a stand (somewhere out on a limb, usually). Some have to do with the removal of influences on pupil growth other than the teacher's behavior; such problems call for familiarity with the proper procedures for analyzing data. None of these problems are insurmountable. And none of them can be solved by abandoning the attempt to measure pupil growth entirely. Yet the attempt has been abandoned in at least 90 per cent of the studies of teacher effectiveness done up to now. In almost every research study in the area, some unvalidated intermediate criterion in the form of judgments or ratings of teacher effectiveness has been used instead of a direct measure of the effects on pupils of the teachers studied.

There is no misconception more deeply rooted in the mind of modern man—layman and professional educator alike—than the notion that it is possible to recognize a good teacher by watching him teach.

Research in teacher effectiveness began with studies in which large numbers of laymen were asked to recall great teachers they had once had, and to tell the investigator what characteristics made them great. The investigator would then classify and summarize these characteristics and publish some sort of a list. Later researchers refined this method by asking only people qualified as experts, a large part of whose *expertise* must have consisted in familiarity with these very same lists, to identify the effective teachers. The final refinement was to have the experts rate teachers' possession of qualities which, according to these same lists, were characteristic of effective teachers. Nowhere in this circular process was there any verification of the assumption that teachers originally judged to be more effective were actually producing greater changes in pupils than teachers identified as less effective.

Recently there have been a few studies which do compare judgments of teacher effectiveness (made by experts) and actual measurements of changes in pupils. Typical conclusions drawn from such studies are:

Teacher rating scales . . . are only slightly related to the observed pupil growth [32].

Correlations between supervisors' ratings and the two measures of growth . . . [were] +.133 and +.067 [42].

. . . evaluations based on . . . supervisors' ratings and those based on measures of pupil growth and achievement were not significantly correlated [6].

. . . supervisory ratings here provided are invalid [as measures of pupil gain] [37].

. . . supervisory ratings . . . seem to lack reliability and validity [as measures of pupil gain] [35].

The criterion of pupil change apparently measures something different than that measured by teacher ratings [30].

The three criteria . . . [pupil gain, pupil evaluations, and a composite of five supervisory ratings] are not related to a greater degree than can be attributed to chance [39].

Whatever pupil gain measures in relation to teaching ability it is not emphasized in supervisory ratings [36a].

Employers' ratings of teaching ability are not related to pupil gains in information [16].

These results may be interpreted as implying that a teacher whose pupils learn almost nothing from him is just about as likely to be rated highly effective as one whose pupils learn a great deal. A characteristic highly correlated with "effectiveness" as judged by a supervisor or other trained person is no more likely to be correlated with measured effectiveness than any other. It is in this sense that studies of effectiveness using judgments of effectiveness as criteria are irrelevant.

Perhaps an outline of what is involved in the measurement of teacher effectiveness will suggest why ratings of effectiveness lack validity. The first step in measuring a teacher's effectiveness is to test his pupils with an achievement test or battery of tests at the beginning and end of a term. Often an aptitude test and a personality test or adjustment inventory are also administered at the beginning of the term. The final achievement score of each individual pupil is then adjusted (by the technique known as analysis of covariance) to make due allowance for any influence that each

Scientific Study of Teacher Behavior

pupil's aptitude, previous learning, and personality or adjustment (as measured by the tests) may have on his final achievement score. Finally, the mean of these adjusted scores of all pupils in each teacher's class is compared with similar means of classes of other teachers (with further adjustments for effects of school and community differences if the classes are in different schools). It is then possible to make statements about the relative effectiveness of the teachers which are called measures of teacher effectiveness.

Would it seem reasonable to ask even the most experienced supervisor to visit a teacher, watch him teach a while, and then judge his effect on even a single pupil—that is, predict the score that pupil would get at the end of the term, making proper allowances for the scores he would get at the beginning of the term? The use of a judgmental criterion would seem to ask the judge to do just this, not for one, but for every pupil in the class, to estimate the mean of all these adjusted scores, and then to compare that mean (with allowances for school and community influences) with similar means for other teachers he may not even have observed.

The belief that an observer can judge a teacher's effectiveness must be based on the idea that by noting the extent to which the teacher behaves in ways known to be effective (or ineffective), the observer can form a judgment of the effect the teacher will probably have on pupils. In other words, the validity of judgmental criteria of teacher effectiveness depends on the assumption that the science of teacher behavior already exists, and studies using such criteria can hardly be expected to contribute much to the birth of the science.

THE PROBLEM OF MEASURING TEACHER BEHAVIOR

When we speak of an effective teacher behavior we do not mean to imply that the behavior was necessarily effective in achieving the teacher's purpose; we judge effectiveness of a behavior in terms of the outcomes we choose to study. This implies the assumption that *the effect of a behavior may not depend on the purpose of the teacher*. Behaviors identical in every respect except the teacher's purpose should have identical effects on the pupils, since the pupils are unaware of the purpose of the teacher so long as it is not manifested externally. What the teacher needs to know to achieve competence is what the probable effect of each behavior is, so that he can exhibit those behaviors which will achieve his purposes most efficiently.

Two behaviors are seldom identical in all observable respects. What would seem to be the same behavior can be quite different in impact according to who exhibits it. This is what the poet had in mind when he characterized the behavior of his mistress by observing that,

> Her very frowns are fairer far
> Than smiles of other maidens are.

The setting or situation in which a behavior occurs also alters its effect. There is a time and a place for everything. Moreover, when a particular teacher does a particular thing at a particular time, it does not necessarily have the same effect on all thirty of his pupils. These three points may be summarized under the heading of the problem of heterogeneity of effects of behavior. If a given behavior had the same effect on every pupil every time it occurred, our task would be simple. It does not and it is not.

The accompanying diagram shows a scheme in which any teacher behavior can be located according to the homogeneity of its effect on pupils. Those behaviors which tend to have the same effect on most pupils when exhibited by most teachers in most situations would fall in Region A. These are the most useful behaviors to know; these behaviors are the ones which should be taught in general methods courses. Perhaps a nice warm smile would fall in Region A.

Behaviors in Region B would be just as useful as behaviors in Region A to certain teachers but worthless to others. If behaviors in Region B are teachable, they must be the result of individualization of instruction in the teacher education program. Probably the individual teacher learns most of these from experience.

Behaviors in Region C are effective with certain types of pupils only. Courses in methods for handling exceptional children should feature this kind of behavior. Research which classifies pupils according to their personality syndromes, levels of intelligence, etc., contributes to our knowledge of behaviors in Region C.

Behaviors in Region D would be contingent upon the classroom situation. Among the many factors which are relevant would be socioeconomic factors in the pupil's background, the particular subject being taught, the type of school organization, and many others.

Region E includes behaviors which are probably not worth trying to teach. If there are any considerable number of behaviors in this region, it follows logically that we will never be able to train teachers to a point where every teacher knows exactly how to behave in every situation with every pupil. If most behaviors fall in Region E, then teaching is an art—and competent teachers are born but not made.

Let us define the over-all effectiveness of any particular behavior as the distance from the origin to its location in the diagram. This means

SCHEME FOR CLASSIFYING TEACHER BEHAVIORS ACCORDING TO HOW OFTEN THEY PRODUCE A PARTICULAR EFFECT

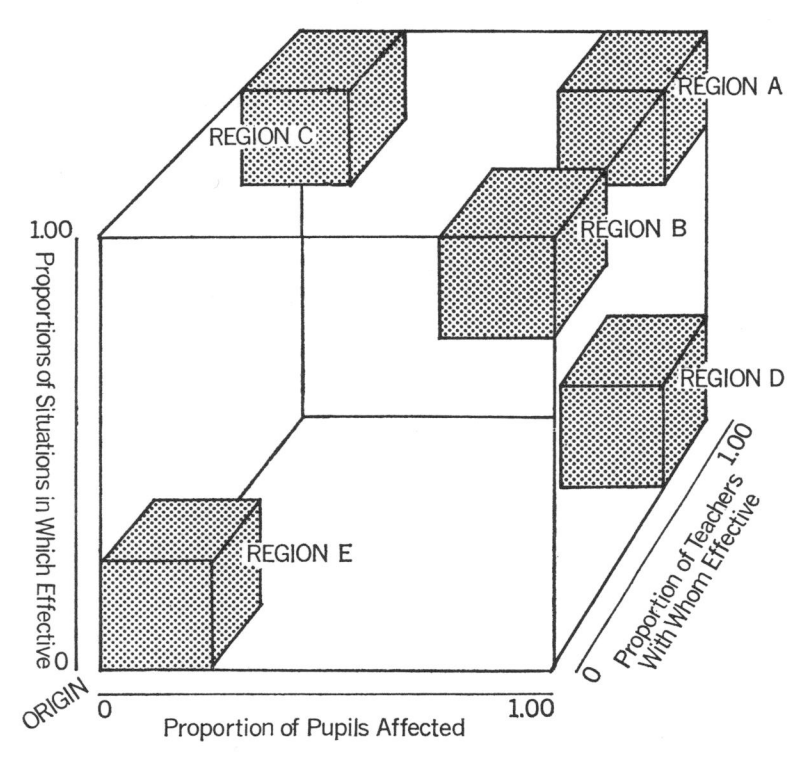

that the most effective behaviors would lie in Region A. Next would be those in Regions B, C, and D. Behaviors in the three unidentified corners would be less effective, and those in Region E would be least effective of all. Effectiveness of a behavior so defined is a function of the total number of teachers, pupils, and situations in which the behavior has a particular effect.

The effectiveness of a behavior could in theory be estimated directly if we could draw a random sample of teachers, pupils, and situations, and count the number of times that behavior was effective. This is not practical because it is impossible to isolate the effects of individual behaviors.

We therefore must fall back on a less direct method. We count the number of times each teacher exhibits the behavior during a certain time, and measure his effectiveness over the same period. Then we try to determine whether the teachers who exhibit the behavior most frequently are the ones who are most effective, in terms of their average effect on all the pupils in their classes. When we do this we assume that behaviors affecting only a few pupils—in Region C, perhaps—will have lower mean effectiveness scores than behaviors in Region A. Thus, less effective behaviors tend to drop out and only the most effective ones remain.

We operate, of course, under the assumption that there are such things as effective behaviors; that is, that not all teacher behaviors are clustered in Region E. A review of past research which has sought to relate effectiveness to behaviors objectively observed and recorded, as contrasted to ratings, suggests that it is difficult to isolate specific behaviors which deviate much from the origin. Region E is by no means empty.

Few behaviors have been identified which are effective in a majority of all the situations in which they occur. A skillful teacher's repertoire may include many different behaviors likely to produce a certain effect, and he selects one or another of them according to his perception of the situation which prevails at a given time. Two teachers who are equally successful in achieving a particular effect may have somewhat different repertoires. We have made the operating assumption that their repertoires will overlap—that both will exhibit some of the same behaviors. These are the behaviors we look for; and these are the behaviors which should be easiest to find.

Most past attempts to measure classroom behavior have failed because of a misconception about behavior measurement which, though less universal than the idea that an effective teacher can be recognized by watching him teach, has done almost as much damage. This is the assumption that teacher behavior can be measured with a rating scale or similar device.

The common approach to the study of the characteristics of effective teachers is to send observers to visit each of a group of teachers and rate each one on a number of behavioral characteristics considered more or less likely to be relevant to effectiveness. Often these ratings are correlated with ratings of over-all competence in an attempt to learn something about the nature of teacher effectiveness.

Some of the problems connected with rating devices are well known. Observer biases, the halo effect, and criterion contamination are familiar adversaries, and there are more or less adequate ways of dealing with them. But trying to obtain objective measures of behavior through ratings is a much more difficult matter.

Measuring behavior with ratings seems to require just about the same sort of superhuman skill on the part of the observer as measuring effectiveness with ratings does—if not more.

If behavior is to be measured objectively through observation—and there seems to be no other way of measuring it—then the task of the observer should be to *record* behavior only. If different behaviors are to be weighted and combined to yield scores which describe the behavior in quantitative terms, this should be done later, by a clerk or a computer. A simple-minded, empirical approach to the problem would be as follows:

Observe a large number of teachers, recording all the behaviors of each one. Measure the effectiveness of each teacher and use item-analysis to discover which behaviors characterize highly effective teachers. Within sampling limits these behaviors may be taken as defining the domain of effective behaviors. Just as no single item in a paper-and-pencil test has a very high validity by itself, so the effectiveness of any individual behavior may not be very high; and just as a test made up of several items rapidly develops validity greater than that of any of the individual items, so the group of items obtained will be more closely related to effectiveness than any one item by itself.

Experience suggests that it may take surprisingly few items to produce a substantial correlation with effectiveness—as few as three or four have been known to suffice.

We have been reluctant to use this approach: when the best three or four items are selected empirically from a pool, the shrinkage in their composite validity on cross-validation is likely to be considerable, unless the pool is very small. A multiple correlation obtained in this way is not an unbiased estimate of the correlation between the selected items and the criterion—it is, in fact, an estimate of the highest correlation that can be obtained with that many items from that pool. In another sample it is not inconceivable that an entirely different set of items might be the ones to yield the highest correlation.

Instead of using this item-analysis approach, we have followed the practice of setting up a priori blocks of items that show some psychological consistency—that seem to "go together"—and which on analysis show high internal consistency; and then correlating the blocks with a criterion of effectiveness. Correlations so obtained are much less likely to overestimate the true correlation and may therefore be expected to stand up better on cross-validation. We have also used factor analysis to locate the most homogeneous subsets of items, before correlating the factor scores with the criterion.

When this works, it results in the identification of effective behavior patterns made up of items not separately effective enough to be detected. Its use is attended by the risk that by combining behaviors in the wrong way we may cover up what we are trying to find. This seems to be a risk we have to take.

THE PRESENT STATUS OF THE SCIENCE

Workable systems for recording at least some aspects of behavior have been in existence almost as long as research in teacher effectiveness has been going on. But it was not until after World War II that studies using objective measurements of classroom behavior began to appear in any number. At Wisconsin, a number of investigations (many of which involved direct observation of teachers) appeared [for example, 32, 35, 37, 39], following lines laid down by Barr [11]. At Illinois, H. H. Anderson and his associates [3, 4, 5], working in the context of child psychology, developed objective measures of emotional climate in nursery and elementary schools. Also at Illinois, but more in the tradition of curriculum research along the lines of Wrightstone's earlier work [61], Cornell and his associates [19] measured differences in classroom behavior in schools of various types in communities of various sizes.

Techniques for the measurement of classroom behavior have been further refined in the past decade or so. Classroom climate is probably the one dimension that has been most successfully measured, the initial work of H. H. Anderson having been advanced by Withall [58], Mitzel and Rabinowitz [45], and Flanders [23]. In our own work we [43] combined the Withall technique with modifications of the Cornell instrument into an instrument called the Observation Schedule and Record (or OScAR) on which three practically orthogonal dimensions of behavior could be scored: Emotional Climate, Verbal Emphasis, Social Organization. Conspicuously absent, however, was any dimension or set of dimensions related to the organization of the content of instruction and the flow of ideas in the lesson. Progress toward the development of dimensions in this area is provided in the work of Muriel Wright and Virginia Proctor [60] in mathematics classes, and that of B. O. Smith [55] in classes in various high school subjects.

The behaviors of teachers while they teach and pupils while they learn are beginning to become objectively quantifiable. Better measures of at least some of the changes in pupil behavior which represent the effects of teacher behavior than have ever been available before are provided by several achievement batteries developed in the forties and fifties. The potentialities which inhere in modern statistical methods for teasing out relationships between behaviors and effects, despite the many irrelevant factors which tend to mask them, are beginning to be realized and exploited; this is, of course, greatly facilitated by modern high-speed computers. Are we on the verge of a major breakthrough in the science of teacher behavior?

STUDY OF CHILDREN THROUGH OBSERVATION OF CLASSROOM BEHAVIOR

EDNA SHAPIRO
Research Division
Bank Street College of Education

THIS REPORT CONCERNS ONE ASPECT OF A LARGE-SCALE RESEARCH UNdertaking designed to assess the psychological impact of differing kinds of school experience on children nine to ten years old.[1] I will summarize some of the data from the observation of classroom behavior, but I want briefly to describe the larger study since its design and concepts have determined the shape and scope of the observational material as well as the direction of the analysis.

The study was conducted in four urban schools selected to represent contrasting educational ideologies; the central dimension of the study, the dimension along which the schools vary, has been designated as the modern-traditional continuum. This is clearly not a simple unitary dimension; nor is it easy to define precisely or succinctly. At the most general level, the schools vary in the extent to which they have been influenced by contemporary thinking about learning and personality development. The modern orientation in education may be characterized as one in which traditional educational goals and methods of teaching and of encouraging learning have been opened to question, and although there may be no uniform answers to the questions, certain values have been stated, certain goals have been clarified, and certain emphases and points of balance have been shifted. Let me try to clarify what we have meant by this concept by

---

[1] This research has been supported by National Institute of Mental Health, grant M-1075, and has been conducted under the general direction of Barbara Biber. The material reported here draws on the work of a number of members of the Bank Street research staff; in particular, Zachary Gussow, Ethel Horn, and Raya Wudowsky have shared responsibility for this aspect of the study.

noting some of the themes which have been seen as central to the modern orientation: The relationship between the teacher and the child is considered a vital part of the educational process; the teacher strives to exert a relatively rational and flexible authority; the child group is itself considered an instrument for planning and learning. It is expected that learning will be facilitated when the curriculum is rooted in content of intrinsic interest to children. Part of the teacher's goal is to enable the child, through his school learning, to experience an increased sense of mastery and positive self-feeling; she tries to see each child as an individual, learning not only the particular skills and content of the curriculum, but also how to find his place in the peer and adult world.

Particular schools and particular teachers differ, of course, in the goals they set, in the way they attempt to carry them out, and in the way they would label their educational values and practices. For the purposes of this study a working definition of the modern educational orientation was considered adequate for the selection of the schools; the schools and classrooms were studied in detail so as to provide extensive documentation of the way these four schools articulate and enact their ideologies.

Three of the schools were selected from a large metropolitan school system; the fourth is an independent experimental school which has for many years exemplified modern educational values. Naturally, it was essential to minimize the effects of extraneous variables that might compete with or cloud over those of central interest. The four schools, while varying on the modern-traditional continuum, are matched effectively in a number of ways: They serve relatively homogeneous populations; have had relatively stable administration and point of view; are reputed to be good schools; are characterized by a reasonably benign attitude toward children; and in all, the task of teaching children is perceived as a serious professional responsibility. The inclusion of a private school necessarily determined the socioeconomic range of the population; consequently, the public schools selected also serve children from well-educated, high-income, middle-class families.

In this study multiple and varied measures have been obtained on a limited number of subjects in a limited number of settings, at a single level of school life—fourth grade. The fourth grade seemed especially appropriate for this study for several reasons: nine-year-old children have attended school for several years and one can therefore presume some cumulative effect of schooling; they are, however, not yet involved in the concerns of preadolescence, nor are they markedly affected by differential rates of sexual maturation.

The four schools were studied in detail in terms of their functioning as social-psychological institutions; extensive observational records were taken in at least one fourth-grade classroom in each school; 105 children from those classrooms were intensively interviewed and individually tested; and the children's mothers answered a questionnaire regarding attitudes to child-rearing and were seen for individual interviews.

The principal of each school was asked to recommend fourth-grade teachers who represented good teaching as defined in his or her school. These teachers were interviewed and their classrooms observed (their willingness to participate was, of course, an essential condition). It was of critical importance that the teacher of the study classroom represent the mainstream of thought and practice in the school; the study class and the study teacher, therefore, were selected to be generally congruent with the school's dominant educational orientation. It is assumed that the influence of the classroom is continuous with that of the school. In spite of the special characteristics of the individual teacher, her idiosyncratic ways of teaching and organizing the children's learning, a basic premise of the study has been that the children reflect less the particular qualities of their current classroom than the cumulative impact of their several years of experience in school.

The classroom is the major arena of interaction between the school and the child; here educational ideology is implemented through specific method and directly affects the child. In this part of the study, the goals have been: (1) to provide descriptive documentation of educational processes, of the nature and quality of children's life in school; (2) to document the congruence of the selected study classroom with the school as a total institution; and (3) to provide descriptive records of study children in naturalistic settings.

Records were taken by three observers who followed a formal schedule, rotating among the four schools. Observations were systematically distributed to cover the range of classroom activities—academic periods, assemblies, gym, elections, discussions, etc. In the course of the two-year period of data-collection, several hundred hours of classroom life were observed.

The need for data relevant to a variety of topics and suitable for different kinds of analyses led to the choice of a narrative-description method of recording which would provide detailed accounts of behavior and interaction without sacrificing the context and sequence of events. Record-taking was governed by a series of observational guides organized into broad categories which provide a framework for recording. These guides prescribe dimensions of significance for the study and detail the kinds of material the observers should focus on in different situations.

The children are the central figures of the records; the observer focused on the class group or on individual children, recording the teacher's behavior primarily to describe the context of the children's behavior. In some records, however, the teacher became the central figure, and in many more records than we had anticipated her behavior was recorded in detail, not because of our primary interest in her teaching methods or style but because of the inescapable salience of the teacher as the center of action and power in the classroom.

In summary, our goal was a set of narrative records which would give behavioral detail set in the context of and related to the stream of events in the classroom.

This rather open method of recording, using a minimum of precoded categories, requires a relatively complex and extended protocol analysis. The concepts governing the analysis of data have been dictated by the general concerns of the larger study. A major theme in the formulation of hypothesized differences between children who have attended relatively modern as opposed to relatively traditional schools has been the children's cognitive functioning and thinking processes. (Parenthetically, may I note that we have not considered the observational data appropriate for testing predictions about the effects of school experience. Clearly, children's behavior in the classroom represents a blend of what the children can do, want to do, and are permitted or encouraged to do. The primary concern of this study has been the assessment of internalized effects of school experience and the observational method by its nature is focused on external behavior. Rather, it was expected that these data would provide supplementary material for the understanding of predictive outcomes, and to the extent that the data do form orderly and coherent patterns, they serve to clarify the implications of the findings.)

A sample of 69 records of academic periods was selected as most appropriate for the analysis of cognition; these records cover the times designated in the curriculum as social studies, language arts, arithmetic—time when the teacher actively directs the children's learning. The periods covered range from fifteen minutes to over an hour; what the children were actually doing varied considerably, both within schools and across schools.

In selecting an appropriate unit of analysis we considered segmenting the records into behavior units or episodes, but decided that for this analysis (and for most other analyses of these data) the total record was the most appropriate unit. Each record represents a natural unit in that an activity period was observed; the time differences reflect actual differences in the length of the particular activity; thus the unit of observation became the unit for analysis.

Observation of Classroom Behavior 95

The analysis was done on masked records: All references, all names or comments, that could identify the school in which the record was taken were deleted (this was first of all a comparative study). Although such masking can never be perfect, and many records could nevertheless easily be identified, this procedure seemed to serve an important function, perhaps mainly in its effect on the mental set of the data-analysts. It helped to focus attention on *what* had transpired and *why,* and to minimize concern with *who;* it also helped in considering each record as a separate datum.

The records have been analyzed from two points of view: in terms of the way the teacher structures the children's cognitive experiences, and in terms of the children's cognitive behavior in group learning situations. We have also made some attempts to put these two kinds of analysis together, to estimate the relation between the teacher's handling of the class and the children's response.

Essentially the method has been one of coding into predetermined, mutually exclusive categories and subsequent rating of more inferential or broader dimensions.

The first analysis focuses on the teacher. Here, the analytic scheme was divided into two sections, each leading to an over-all rating. We tried to keep the subvariables rooted in behavior, but several of them also require inferential judgment. The two basic ratings made are: *emphasis on relationship thinking,* and *leeway allowed for independent cognitive exploration.* It is clear that these are not independent, conceptually unrelated dimensions. They are, however, not perfectly correlated and the behavioral cues used in judging and rating are somewhat different.

The category judgments which bear on the assessment of emphasis on *relationship thinking* tend to be concerned with teaching method, with the teacher's approach to communicating information, with the kinds of learning she apparently values. The rater categorized each record in the following terms:

In her approach to the mastery of symbolic skills does the teacher emphasize memorization, repetitive drill, exercises? Or does she emphasize understanding principles, making logical connections?

In her approach to the mastery of conceptual knowledge, does she encourage research skills—skill in reporting, in evaluating others, in listening, in answering? Or does she encourage conceptualization—putting together ideas, taking discrete facts another step, looking for connections, probing meanings?

In her orientation to problem solving, does she provide step-by-step directions for the solution of a given problem? Or does she give children an opportunity to try out ideas which would lead to problem solution, let them find the problem?

This is rather a condensed summary, offering either/or choices; the steps in the coding schema are not presented in detail, partly for brevity, partly because the crude realities of research practice require pooling and condensing so that, in general, the statistical testing was done in this either/or way. The ratings are based on but do not follow directly from the component categories; the rater was free to synthesize and weigh in order to arrive at an over-all judgment.

Something of what is meant by relationship thinking should be clearer now. It is a shorthand expression for an approach to learning—especially, in this connection, to teaching—that stresses the search for interrelationships among facts and ideas; that attempts to foster understanding by relating facts and concepts to known experience; that allows, expects, complexity and even confusion to precede resolution; that accepts relative and conditional statements; that tolerates the ambiguity of the presolution period in thinking. It is here opposed to a more fact-centered, product-oriented approach that places greater stress on speed, accuracy, and the conclusive mastery of known, established, and accepted modes of thinking and of solution.

The categories relevant to assessing *the leeway the teacher allows for independent cognitive exploration* tend to concern the learning-teaching climate the teacher creates and the nature of the content she introduces and accepts. There is an assumption here that certain conditions are conducive to independent thinking, or, to keep it in terms of what the teacher does, certain conditions indicate that she allows, encourages, the children's individual independent attempts.

Is the pace she allows consonant with that of the children—does she accept their pace, allow them time to complete tasks? Or is it dissonant—does she hurry the children, do they wait for her?

Is the content of the subject matter she introduces close to or distant from the children's realm of experience?

Is the scope of content she accepts as relevant broad or narrow?

Is the atmosphere for learning generated by the teacher task-oriented and harmonious, or is it centered on maintenance of order, or is it tense?

What role does she take vis-à-vis the children's thinking:

Do her remarks and comments tend to support the children's thinking—does she pick up cues, extend their ideas? Or do her remarks tend to interfere with or interrupt the children?

Does she assist them when they seem to need it—give active

assistance or emotional support when they flounder? Or does she ignore them, insist they work out problems for themselves?

Again, there is no direct one-to-one relationship between the category judgments and the rating; the rating subsumes the categories, but is more general. Both terms—independent and exploration—are crucial. The rating is an attempt to assess the extent to which the teacher, through the learning situation she creates, allows and/or encourages the children to think for themselves and to think in open, sometimes idiosyncratic ways, bringing in their own associations and experiences, rather than leading or even guiding them to a predetermined end point.

These judgments were made by three raters who independently categorized and rated all 69 records. Reliability measures are based on an average rating per classroom rather than record by record, and were calculated by an analysis of variance procedures. The reliability of the two major ratings is .90 and .94. For the nine sets of category judgments, the correlations range from .51 to .99; only one is so low (and that has the lowest *N* of all judgments), the next is .74, and the median is .89. This seems a respectable array of reliability coefficients and in subsequent analyses only two raters, or sample checks, were used.

For the purposes of this study we were interested in comparing the thinking-learning situation in terms of the basic study continuum. It was necessary to combine records from the two traditional and the two modern schools in order to make statistical comparisons. Differences between the two sets of schools along these dimensions are consistent and statistically significant. While we know that each school, each classroom, is different, and some of the differences within pairs are meaningful and discernible, for the most part, differences between the pairs are so great that differences within are obscured. This is itself an interesting fact since the criteria for selection of schools were rather stringent and the study schools are in many important ways alike, especially if one considers the wide range of possible schools in even an urban situation. Our coding schema point to some interesting and useful dimensions, but the system is not highly refined; rather gross criteria serve to discriminate the traditional from the modern classroom along these dimensions. If one were dealing with a narrower sample of schools, or perhaps attempting comparisons of classrooms within a school, a more highly differentiated set of categories might be required.

As I have indicated, the two pairs of schools are clearly differentiated. Chi-square tests yield *p* values less than .01 or .02 for all comparisons using category judgments. The differences between means on the two major ratings were tested by analysis of variance and in both cases the modern schoolrooms are clearly differentiated from the more traditional in the expected direction ($p < .01$). (The t-test comparisons of the individual classes are also significant, but unfortunately the N for one of the traditional schools is too low to allow separate comparison.)

There is one other aspect of this analysis I would like to mention. In analyzing the sample of 69 records, not all categories were applicable to each record—the categories "does not apply" and "insufficient data" were perforce often used. For the nine sets of category judgments, the Ns range from 16 in one case to 60 (the median is 37); the two ratings, being more general, could be made on 58 (84 per cent) and 62 (90 per cent) of the records, respectively. In some cases, this is to be expected—certain judgments were not pertinent to all records, e.g., the evaluation of approach to symbolic skills applies to periods when arithmetic and language were being taught. In other cases, the number of records yielding sufficient relevant data to make a judgment offers some information about the generality of the concept. The question of what level of generality is most meaningful and fruitful plagues every research undertaking. Looking back, it is easy to see that some dimensions should have been more differentiated, while in other instances certain distinctions could have been eliminated. The two categories that have the highest Ns are pace ($N = 60$) and closeness or distance of the subject matter ($N = 50$). Certainly there are few teaching situations without pace or subject matter. One category that has a low N (21) also has the lowest reliability: approach to conceptual knowledge. Here I suspect that these two facts reflect some fuzziness of conceptualization. But before using this index of generality to throw out excess or weak coding categories, note that the category with the smallest number of applicable records is one of the most interesting: the scope of content accepted (by the teacher) as relevant. One can see that there would be many situations where such a judgment simply could not be made, but it seems a most important concept, and when the relevant data are present, the judgment apparently can be made with some consistency (reliability coefficient is .74 which is not bad for 16 records).

I would like to turn now, briefly, to the parallel analysis of the records from the point of view of the *children's cognitive behavior*. Two raters analyzed the same 69 records from this point of view.[2] A sample of 17 records was selected for a reliability check. Again, reliability was

---

[2] It should be noted that there was a lapse of time, filled by other work, between the two analyses. The previous ratings were of course not available and the records were masked; the raters felt that they did not remember judgments and ratings previously assigned to particular records.

computed on average ratings per classroom. In spite of the small number of cases, reliability coefficients are rather high (the lowest is .67, the highest .99, the median .97).

The nature of the children's cognitive functioning has been a major focus in this study, and a good deal of material has been gathered on the children's performance in individual tests, interviews, on group achievement and intelligence tests. Describing and assessing their functioning in the classroom situation was, therefore, of paramount interest. But it was not so easy to find ways of getting at it.

Thinking is by nature elusive and implicit; observation is by nature external, molar. We do not purport to make statements about the children's thinking from these data; we can make some judgments of the characteristics of their verbalized thoughts, some about the quality of their apparent motivation. We tried, perhaps we should have known better at the outset, to assess their competence or adequacy in the classroom, and ratings were made, only to be put aside as inadequate and incompetent. The nature of the tasks set for the children, the teacher's requirements and expectations, differed so from classroom to classroom that it was impossible to apply consistent standards. If one then tries to take into account the difficulty of the questions posed for the children, one becomes involved in a complex and suspect weighting game.

The analysis of children's cognitive behavior concerns two major topics: *Involvement* and *Quality of Thinking*.

The major dimension, *involvement in work, learning, and ongoing activities,* was rated on a five-point scale. The rating was based on an extensive cue list which includes such factors as desire to participate, content of participation, content of child-child interaction (i.e., task-related or extraneous to task), amount of time spent in actual work, the children's apparent feeling, etc. Some of these subratings and category judgments received separate treatment while others could not be dealt with separately. We were trying to get at *intrinsic* involvement in work and learning, not busyness, general activity, involvement in one's own non-class-related activity, doing several things simultaneously. Significant differences were obtained: Children in the traditional school classrooms were rated as less involved than those in the modern school room, and the differences are sustained in individual comparisons ($p < .01$).

In attempting to assess the quality of the children's *thinking,* may I repeat that we were limited here to what the children said, and of course what they said was very often a response to what they were asked. And very often what they were asked does not allow much scope for thinking. The children's contributions were evaluated along three dimensions:

relevance of their statements, coherence of their statements, and quality of their thinking, especially with respect to evidence of relationship thinking. There are no differences with respect to relevance and coherence; most statements in all classrooms were rated as relevant and coherent. There are differences in the extent and quality of their relationship thinking, a dimension which forms a natural parallel to the earlier analysis of teacher-structuring and to the independent analysis of their cognitive functioning in individual problem tasks. In evaluating the children's thinking and the quality of their reasoning, a broad scope of content was considered relevant—instances where the children attempt to make connections, introduce ideas, pertinent observations, offer comments or ask thoughtful questions, as well as when they are working on problems.

The records were rated on a three-point scale (the condensation of the scale reflects the nature of the data, not of the phenomenon). Significant differences were obtained: The children in the traditional school classrooms were rated as showing less evidence of relationship thinking than those in the modern school classrooms, and the differences are sustained in individual comparisons ($p < .01$).

One might say that if the first analysis of the teacher showed little encouragement of relationship thinking, naturally the analysis of the children would show little evidence—the children had less opportunity. I mentioned that we have attempted to put together these two analyses—of the teacher's role in creating a climate of thinking, and of the children's response. This analysis is tentative and incomplete and I can only hint at what it suggests. By simply making scatter plots using the two sets of ratings, or ratings and judgments, one can easily see the relation of, say, the evaluation of the teacher's encouragement of relationship thinking to the quality of the children's thinking. They are of course highly correlated, but not perfectly, and the patterns for some of these plots suggest differences from class to class that are of interest. One gets a very clear picture of the differences in variability from classroom to classroom; one of the classrooms has notably more variability and it is that of the modern public school, which is exactly where one would expect to find it. Further, in the two traditional school rooms there is a tendency for the children to be functioning on a somewhat higher level than the teacher is asking for. Other sources of data in this study corroborate the notion that these children are capable of a much higher level of performance than they are engaged in or asked for in their ordinary school work.

I do not feel that our analyses of the teacher's role and of the children's functioning match the subtlety and range the teacher can bring to her job, nor the subtlety required of educators and psychologists in

Observation of Classroom Behavior 101

thinking about the place and function of the school in helping children develop their power as thinking individuals. But it seems a line of inquiry worth pursuing. The teacher introduces the children to the world of thought through the kinds of rules and rituals with which she surrounds the thinking process; the kinds of content she introduces, accepts, and rejects from the children; the kinds of approaches to problem solution she encourages and sustains; the amount of freedom she allows for independent and exploratory thinking; the speed with which she closes down inquiry; the respect she shows for their fumbling, their confusion—all create for them an image of that world and a set of expectations about their own potency as learners and thinkers.

ANALYSIS OF TWO KINDERGARTEN SETTINGS

MARTIN KOHN
Research Division
Bank Street College of Education

THE WORK TO BE REPORTED HERE IS THE BY-PRODUCT OF AN INTENSIVE pilot study on the relationship between the child's role in school and his role in the home at the beginning of his school life, namely, during his kindergarten year.[1] One of the major underlying concepts is the assumption that a classroom is not a homogeneous setting but rather a multiplicity of places which children can fill, and the specific spot which a child comes to occupy and the specific role which he comes to play will be jointly determined by the niches available in a particular classroom and the kind of selection that the child makes on the basis of his personality. It is further assumed that there will be some degree of correspondence, on a dynamic level, between the place the child selects in the classroom and the place which he occupies in the family constellation.

In this study a relatively small number of children was followed for a period of an entire school year. The children were tested and the parents interviewed several months before the beginning of school. After entry into school, the children were observed in the classrooms and further interviews were held with the parents throughout the kindergarten year. The main emphasis of the observations in the classrooms was twofold: (*a*) observations of the individual children who were being studied intensively, and (*b*) observations of the classrooms themselves in order to describe them as settings in which these children functioned.

The over-all design of the study called for following the children in

[1] This research has been supported by grant 3M-9135 from the National Institute of Mental Health, U.S. Public Health Service. The author gratefully acknowledges the work of Mrs. Evelyn Levinrew and Mrs. Harriet Deck who carried out the classroom observations, and Mrs. Comilda Weinstock who is carrying major responsibility in the analysis of the data.

two classrooms, preselected for their marked contrast. The teacher in Classroom A was oriented toward providing a varied program of play and activity based on child interests at this stage of development. The teacher in Classroom B enacted a more rigid program, with more clearly defined tasks, of which the underlying purpose was to prepare the children for their future school life.

The following report is an attempt to highlight the conceptual framework and methodology being developed for the description and mental health assessment of these two classrooms. It is anticipated that the ideas and methods will undergo further tests and refinement in future, more extensive, work.

The conceptualization of the classroom proceeded from the following definition: that the classroom is a social-psychological system which exists for the enactment of educational goals. This definition has the following central implications for conceptualization as well as methodology:

(*a*) Since its function is the enactment of educational goals, the concepts and analytic categories would have to reflect in some definite way the transactions which are germane to teaching and learning; in other words, a generalized scheme of analysis, such as the Bales Interaction System [9a], would not fit the requirement.

(*b*) Since it is a social-psychological system, the participation of all the members of the system would have to be taken into account, the child as well as the teacher: how the system organizes and maintains itself (the general area of classroom management), by what norms and values the conduct of teacher and pupils is regulated, what social structures are established, certain over-all aspects such as the intellectual and emotional climate of the system, and so on.

The work to date on these two classrooms has been limited to a few of the implications of this conception. The role of the teacher has been examined in its major aspects of structuring, assisting, and evaluating and, within this, whether she directed herself to the play and work activities or to maintaining order in the classroom. The second point of focus has been on the children's role in participating in the classroom process, then interactions with one another and their response to the teacher in her various functions.

Data in these two classrooms were collected at four different periods during the school year. The concepts and methods will be illustrated by analysis of data, gathered during the first two months of school; the data are based on teacher-focused and group-focused observations of one half-hour duration. For the teacher observations, the main focus of the observers was to follow her through her activities and record her actions, at the same time including as much of the group's functioning as was necessary for recording response as well as context. For the group observations the observers recorded activities for the total group of children or, when it was split up into subgroups, systematically rotated among these.

The decision was made that the observations were to be nonselective; the observers were asked to record as much as possible of what was occurring within the foci of activity. The rationale for making nonselective observations was: (a) these data were to be used to develop and refine the conceptual and methodological ideas, and (b) findings yielded by the analysis were at all points to be informally compared and contrasted to phenomenological appraisal of these classrooms, in order to determine intuitive validity.

The instructions to the observers were briefly as follows: to report as much detail as was meaningful on a molar level, to report meaningful sequences and follow behavioral episodes to their end, to report the quality of behavior, and to denote time at approximately five-minute intervals.

The half-hour observations were further subdivided into units of activity, such as free play, art, rest, playground. The subdivision of the records into these natural units was done for two reasons: (a) to apply a more detailed analysis to units which would be functionally meaningful, and (b) to have some basis for comparison between the two classrooms, that is, to be able to pick a sample of two comparable records, one from each classroom, for each of the activity units.

All the observations made on one particular day of the week during the first observation period were unitized and seven matched units were selected for each of the two classrooms. Specifically, these units were: arrival, easel, milk, rest, playground, music, and art. These seven units represent approximately two hours of classroom time in Classroom B, and approximately three hours of classroom time in Classroom A. All data reported subsequently are equalized for time.

Each of these units was further analyzed using categories falling under the following general topics.

Structuring: extent to which the teacher structured for general over-all goals; extent to which she structured in a step-by-step fashion in terms of sub-aims of the activity; extent to which she structured for specificity of details, etc.

Assistance: extent to which the teacher volunteered assistance; extent to which she gave or refused assistance in response to children's request for it, etc.

Evaluation: extent to which the teacher made approving or disapproving statements; extent to which the approving statements were superficial or meaningful; extent to which the disapproving statements were constructive or destructive.

Analysis of Two Kindergarten Settings

Child selectivity and initiative: extent to which the children freely varied the timing of the next step, either initiating the activity, terminating it, or proceeding freely within it; extent to which the teacher intervened when the child so proceeded.

Child-child interactions: extent to which the children interacted with each other; whether they structured for each other, evaluated each other, assisted each other, worked or played with each other in a cooperative way.

Children's involvement: extent to which the children gave evidence of being involved in classroom activities in a positive way, that is, showed signs of pleasure or interest, or in a negative way, showing signs of tensions or restlessness; extent to which the children gave evidence of experiencing difficulty.

All the child-child interactions were simultaneously scored as to whether they were directly related to the central activity or task of the unit, parallel or counter to it, or whether they occurred in the teacher's presence or absence. The purpose here was to see to what extent the children's relationship to each other was channeled in the direction of the classroom activities, to what extent they could freely interact in social interchange in ways not directly related to these activities, and to what extent their interactions ran counter to what the teacher had structured for.

Furthermore, all the teacher actions, as well as a number of categories of child action, were scored for their primary focus, for example, in "assistance," whether or not the teacher assisted the children in their play or work activities or in "self-help" areas such as dressing and going to the bathroom. In "structuring," a score was made when the teacher structured the activities, or structured for basic orderliness (by basic orderliness is meant whatever is involved in keeping routines as defined by the teacher going)—where and how to sit, when and when not to talk, not to wander around. For "evaluation," whether the teacher approved or disapproved the children's activities was scored, as well as her approval or disapproval of their manners and personal habits. The total number of categories and subcategories utilized was approximately one hundred.

For each of these categories and subcategories, a count of the frequency of occurrence of events falling into it was made. For example, for the subcategory "teacher's step-by-step structuring of classroom activities," a count was made of the number of times this kind of structuring occurred; similarly for positive and negative evaluation, the frequency with which the teacher evaluated in an approving way and in a disapproving way was noted. Counting of frequencies occurred throughout, with three exceptions. These pertain to items which, on an a priori basis, we would expect to happen only once per activity unit, namely, the extent to which the teacher gave the children a choice with regard to determining the activity, the stringency of conditions the teacher stated for participation in an activity, and the extent to which the teacher structured for a general goal rather than for specific subaims of the activity.

The decision to count the frequency of occurrence of events relative to various aspects of classroom life was in part based on dissatisfaction with rating procedures. When ratings are made on the spot, the task facing the observer-rater is an overwhelming one. The multitude of events—some relative to one concept, some to another, some to be rated and synthesized in one way, others rated and synthesized in another way—creates a burdening, if not overtaxing, task; the high intercorrelation among scales may be a reflection of the difficulty of the task as much as of the actual possibility that classroom events can be accounted for by a few basic factors.

A similar criticism may apply to ratings made from observation records. Here a halo effect from knowledge of the total record may enter as a bias into the ratings of specific dimensions, thus exaggerating intercorrelations among dimensions.

Analysis of the classroom based on a frequency count has the advantage of giving a direct and straightforward assessment of the available evidence. Furthermore, it may turn out to be useful in keeping separate and differentiated the many facets of classroom life relevant to a particular conceptual scheme. It was felt that a more articulated picture that would do justice to the complexity of classrooms might be possible through this method.

For the present field work these advantages outweighed a recognized disadvantage of analyzing narrative records by frequency count: unless the area focus of the observation has been predetermined, it is possible that the record of observation will not present an accurate representation of the frequency of occurrence of the items of behavior selected for analysis.

Some brief highlights of the results obtained to date will now be presented. These results are still tentative, and further refinements of data analysis are being carried out at the present time.

On the three items that were rated rather than counted, it was found that (a) the teacher in Classroom A tended to structure for general goals to a much greater extent than the teacher in Classroom B; (b) the teacher in Classroom B tended to state much more stringent conditions for participation in the activity and tended to exercise much greater control over decision making, that is, tended to a much lesser extent to give the children a choice of what they wanted to do.

On those aspects of classroom life that were counted,[2] we find the following:

Structuring	Number of Instances	
	Classroom A	Classroom B
Structuring activities in a step-by-step fashion	5	44
Structuring for specific details	12	28
Structuring by minimal cues and signals	1	12
Structuring for basic orderliness	28	21

In Classroom A we find a lower amount of total structuring; when all instances listed above are combined, there are 46 instances of structuring in Classroom A and 105 in Classroom B; of all the structuring instances, the percentage directed to the activities was considerably less in Classroom A (39 per cent) than in Classroom B (80 per cent).

Group Response to Teacher Structuring	Number of Instances	
	Classroom A	Classroom B
The group response is immediate and complete	0	28
Group responds to teacher structuring, but at its own pace	8	0
The group disregards the teacher's structuring	3	0

It is evident that the group responded in a much more decisive manner in Classroom B than in Classroom A. The much lower over-all frequencies for Classroom A is in part accounted for by the lesser extent to which this teacher structured for the whole group; her tendency was to direct a greater proportion of her structuring to individuals.

Nature and Extent of Assistance	Number of Instances	
	Classroom A	Classroom B
Assistance asked from teacher and assistance given whether requested or not	10	18

The evidence above indicates that a higher frequency of assistance given and/or asked for occurred in Classroom B. In the analysis these figures were further broken down and it was found that in Classroom B the teacher provided assistance when it was required less often than in Classroom A (63 per cent versus 90 per cent).

[2] This procedure ultimately requires an evaluation of reliability in terms of the representativeness of the frequencies of the specific unit periods studied, as well as the degree of interscorer agreement regarding classification of instances into categories.

While the evidence is slight, there is indication that the extent to which these teachers fostered the children's assistance of each other is compatible with this trend:

	Number of Instances	
Encouraging child-child assistance	2	0
Discouraging child-child assistance	0	4

	Number of Instances	
Child Initiative	CLASSROOM A	CLASSROOM B
Total child initiative (total number of instances where children initiated a next step either in their activities or in any other area of classroom life)	112	84
Total child initiative directed to the teacher (again in relation to activities or any other areas; these instances are included in above total)	18	23
Routinized responses (responses that look spontaneous but had been previously trained by the teacher)	5	23

When total child initiative is further broken down into areas, we find that exclusive of the initiative directed toward the teacher, the proportion relating directly to the work and play is fairly similar (52 per cent in Classroom A versus 56 per cent in Classroom B). A higher proportion in Classroom B is directed to the teacher and it is exclusively work-oriented. In Classroom A, on the other hand, only about half of the initiative directed to the teacher is activity-oriented. A relatively lower per cent in Classroom B than in Classroom A of child initiative is directed to "basic orderliness"; in other words, more of the children's energy was directed toward work in Classroom B than in Classroom A.

A further breakdown was made to determine the proportion of child initiative in which the teacher intervenes. Here we find a much higher proportion of intervened responses in Classroom B than in Classroom A (40 per cent versus 5 per cent).

	Number of Instances	
Children's Involvement in Work	CLASSROOM A	CLASSROOM B
Mention of involvement	67	44
Children experiencing difficulty	3	11

The data indicate that the observers picked up more instances of involvement in Classroom A than in Classroom B; the reason for this is

Analysis of Two Kindergarten Settings

not clear. But when involvement was classified into positive and negative, a sharp difference in the distribution emerged, with 11 per cent of the instances in Classroom A being negative (children showing tension or restlessness) and 54 per cent of instances of negative involvement in Classroom B.

The frequency of the different categories is to be considered highly analytic and atomistic indicators of various aspects of classroom functioning. In some instances, these indicators are meaningful in and of themselves; for example, the large number of step-by-step structuring that occurs in Classroom B, the high percentage of child-initiated, nonintervened responses in Classroom A, immediately tell us something about differences in these two settings. However, for most of these major concepts, the indicators need to be synthesized. The synthetic use of the indicators will be illustrated with the following concepts: organization of learning, work orientation, routinization, centrality of the teacher, availability of assistance.

One of the main questions we wanted to answer was the nature of the *organization of learning.* How does the flow of activities proceed in these two classrooms? There are four major alternatives here: (*a*) the teacher structures for over-all objectives to a large extent and gives the children a great deal of leeway to proceed on their own within these over-all objectives, (*b*) the teacher states over-all objectives and does a great deal of specific step-by-step structuring, thus exercising a great deal of control, (*c*) the teacher fails to state over-all objectives and structures primarily in a step-by-step fashion, and (*d*) the teacher neither states over-all objectives nor does specific structuring. Our analysis has indicated that in Classroom A, to a greater extent than in Classroom B, over-all objectives are stated and the children are relatively free to proceed on their own. In Classroom B there is a smaller extent of over-all structuring but a very high extent of step-by-step direction. Relevant to these conclusions are the two teachers' ratings on structuring for over-all objectives, the relative frequency of step-by-step structuring, the total amount of specific structuring, the frequency of nonintervened child initiative.

The question arises whether, within the relatively freer structure of Classroom A, the children are at all related to the work of the classroom. This brings up the topic of degree of *work orientation.* It is clear from the data presented that, even though the structure is freer, a relatively high percentage of children's initiative in Classroom A is focused on the work, although it is not as high as in Classroom B. In Classroom B, 83 per cent of the children's initiative is work related, as compared to 60 per cent in

Classroom A. Other evidence, under teacher structuring and assistance, further indicates the higher degree of work relatedness in Classroom B than in Classroom A.

The next concept is that of degree of *routinization of classroom life*. The degree of routinization seems to be higher in Classroom B than in Classroom A. The teacher in Classroom B exercises control via reduced cues and signals to a much higher degree than the teacher in Classroom A. There is also much more evidence of children making routinized responses in Classroom B than in Classroom A, and they tend to respond in a more immediate way to the teacher's structuring in Classroom B.

A further concept which is of importance is that of *centrality of the teacher*. In Classroom B the children are less free to proceed on their own and a higher percentage of their self-initiated responses are directed toward the teacher. The responses initiated toward the teacher are almost exclusively work related. Furthermore, this teacher tends to limit child-child assistance. Stepping outside the analysis for a moment, we know that this teacher puts a great deal of emphasis on self-reliance; one of the reasons she gives for limiting the children helping each other is that "You should learn to do things by yourself." And, in fact, she controls the work in such a specific way that she makes the children highly dependent on her. In this classroom, the teacher holds the central position; in Classroom A, the children are freer to proceed on their own and are freer to turn to their peers for help and/or guidance.

This brings us to the last concept, namely, the *over-all amount of assistance* available in the classroom. In Classroom B, the teacher tends to refuse help much more often than in Classroom A; she also tends to limit the children in helping each other. In Classroom A, more help is forthcoming from the teacher and the teacher facilitates and encourages children to help each other. Therefore, it is clear that the over-all amount of assistance available to children in Classroom A is greater than in Classroom B.

We would expect that under the more stringent conditions operating in Classroom B, a different picture of work involvement and difficulty with the work would emerge from that which we see in Classroom A. That this is so, in fact, can be seen from the evidence previously presented, namely that the observers noted a higher percentage of positive involvement in Classroom A and a greater number of negative involvements in Classroom B. Also, the observers noted more instances of children having difficulty with the work in Classroom B than in Classroom A.

The procedure so far has involved two steps—the assessment of the evidence (frequency counts of the events falling into the different

Analysis of Two Kindergarten Settings

categories) and the synthesis of these indicators into the concepts relevant to the theoretical scheme. These then are the descriptive steps of the analysis. Two further questions can now be asked. How do these two classrooms function as systems, using as the criterion the fact that their main purpose is the enactment of educational goals? How good are they for children's development?

As far as the first question is concerned, it must suffice here to note that certain of the indicators can be considered as "symptoms." For example, the large number of difficulties and the low degree of positive involvement in Classroom B may be considered a type of disfunctioning of the system, related, on a dynamic level, and among other things, to the extreme degree of step-by-step and specific structuring. In a parallel way, a relatively higher degree of initiative directed to maintaining basic orderliness (in other words to acting up and not paying attention to the main activity) in Classroom A may be indicative of some degree of chaos, related possibly to the looser structuring of that classroom. In other words, certain of the indicators can be considered as symptoms indicative of the extent to which classroom activity is being channeled toward work, of the degree of tension accumulating in the system, etc. These symptoms can therefore be thought of as having a dynamic relationship to other features of the functioning system.

As far as the second question is concerned, we are in the process of working out procedures for applying developmental concepts and criteria to the descriptive categories. Before the beginning of the present program, the Bank Street staff had elaborated a series of mental health criteria applicable to childhood and education (see "Schools and Mental Health Program," Working Paper No. 2, May 1958 [mimeographed]).

In the development of the procedures for the description and assessment of the classroom, we have made an attempt to separate this value orientation, this third step, from the descriptive phases. Even with the best intentions, the separations of the evaluative from the descriptive is never completely feasible. However, within our present procedures, anyone is free to coordinate the indicators to his own set of descriptive concepts or to take the concepts and ascribe to them whatever significance he wishes as far as the functioning of classroom systems and the development of children are concerned.

CLASSROOM PROCESSES STUDY

ELEANOR LEACOCK
Research Division
Bank Street College of Education

THE PURPOSE OF THE CLASSROOM PROCESSES STUDY[1] IS TO DEVELOP A method of analyzing classroom life which will reveal its more important implications for children's growth and learning and by the same token reveal possibilities for the introduction of beneficial changes. Thus the study aims to yield deeper insight into the nature of classroom life, as revealed in observation and interview material on a series of classrooms. In the analysis of our data we have separated out of the complex interrelations of classroom life what we feel to be three fundamental aspects of the way in which motivation for learning is transmitted to children in a school setting:

    1. The way in which the curriculum challenges (or fails to challenge) the interest of children and the extent to which it does (or does not) have meaning for them

    2. The extent to which value is (or is not) placed on learning by the teacher, through direct goal setting and other value-laden statements; through the content of her techniques for evaluating work and for regulating behavior; and through the differential allocation of reward or blame to different children

    3. The way in which learning is reinforced (or undermined) by how the teacher structures the children's relations to her and to each other

    Our analysis of classroom life is based on three sources—observa-

---

[1] This study is supported by National Institute of Mental Health, grant 3M–9135. The research team of the Classroom Processes Study is headed by Eleanor Leacock, and consists of Rosa Graham, Phyllis Gunther, Robert Harrison, Sylvia Knopp, Lisa Peattie, Julius Trubowitz, and Eleanor Wenkart. All team members have participated in the collection of data and in the development of study research design and procedures, in collaboration with senior staff members of the Bank Street College Schools and Mental Health Program.

tions, teacher interviews, and child interviews. The observations are central and take the form of narrative records. Narrative recording was agreed upon both because of the exploratory nature of the study, and because of our multidimensional approach. Interaction can now be coded with reasonable success, but we needed in addition the actual content of the curriculum, and of the values overtly presented by the teacher.

The observational data covered a relatively short time span (three periods of one and a half hours each) since other studies have indicated a high reliability for the analysis of teacher performance from relatively short periods of classroom observation. However, although taken over a brief period, records are extremely intensive and detailed. Two observers recorded simultaneously, one concentrating on the teacher and her teaching and classroom management techniques, and the other on the children's responses, the style of their interaction, and general classroom atmosphere. Although the presence of observers "tones down" certain behavior, nonetheless the basic characteristics of the classroom, as we are analyzing them, come through. The two records were written up as one running account. Shortly after the observation, each observer rated the teacher and students along some twenty dimensions, after which concensus ratings were arrived at through discussion.

The teacher was interviewed both before and after the observations, using a schedule which enabled us to get consistent information on all classrooms, but open-ended enough to allow the teacher to elaborate on her own interests, attitudes, and understanding of her teaching and of the children. The child interview was short and direct, eliciting straightforward answers from the children about what school meant to them, how they were doing, what the teacher liked and disliked, etc. The fact that the children presumably answered what they felt they "should" in no way diminishes the significance of the interview; this is precisely what we wanted.

After preliminary visits to a number of schools, we undertook a full-scale pilot study of one second grade. Following this, the middle second and middle fifth grades in four schools were selected for intensive study. In order to look at classrooms in the context of known and demographically definable differences in school experiences for children, involving different expectations for performance, different relations to authority, and different out-of-school experiences, schools were chosen in four relatively homogeneous but socioeconomically contrasting neighborhoods: a middle-income Negro neighborhood, a lower-income Negro neighborhood, a middle-income white neighborhood, and a lower-income white neighborhood.

Analysis of observational and interview material has proceeded along several lines, according to what is warranted by the limitations of the material and the nature of the findings sought. Procedures include simple analysis or description of certain dimensions, intensive analysis and discussion of others, frequency counts of incidents categorized according to several dimensions, simple collation of incidents or statements, and correlations among various data.

The basic analytic instrument which incorporates these data is an "Outline for the Characterization of a Classroom." The outline is comprised of four sections:

    1. Background data: descriptive and demographic material on the school and classrooms

    2. The basic first level analysis of observation and interview data on the classroom

    3. A summary statement of the characteristics of a given classroom drawn from the previous section and along the lines described at the beginning of this report

    4. A hypothetical statement about the directions in which a given classroom would appear to enable or inhibit the intellectual and social growth of children

The second and basic section of the outline deals separately with material on the teacher and on the children, and for each has three further subdivisions: (*a*) the curriculum itself, (*b*) the structure of social relations in the classroom, and (*c*) behavioral modes and stated attitudes as revealed in both observations and interviews. When dealing with how the teacher manages the classroom, we have differentiated between the formal arrangements and rules and routines, and informal structuring, or the teacher's enactment of her rules, including the style, content, and differential allocation of her interest, attention, encouragement or praise, and criticism or punishment.

The third and summary section of the outline synthesizes this material along the lines of the three main study foci: the curriculum itself, the value placed on learning by the teacher, and the way in which the teacher's structuring reinforces or undermines learning.

The curriculum itself. We have a number of ratings on the teacher's presentation of the curriculum, evaluating its "flexibility," "variability," "originality," and so forth. We also have a frequency count on the extent to which the teacher "closes" an incident, however supportively, or "opens it up" for further exploration. However, the most important item on the curriculum is a long analytic description based on full discussion of the record not only by the observers but also by experienced consultants available at the College. We analyze the curriculum along the following lines:

1. Nature and clarity of the teacher's concept of teaching, particularly with regard to the integration and development of curriculum
2. Relation of content to children's experiences
3. Depth, richness, and variety
4. Style of learning and thought (development of "adventurous" and/or "systematic" thinking; practice in routine skills; nature of involvement in thought process)
5. Value content of material from teacher's statements, texts and displays

The teacher interviews are subjected to scrutiny along the same lines by a team of two, including someone other than the teacher interviewer, and the results are combined or compared to give a full picture of what the children are being asked to learn, and how.

The value placed on learning by the teacher. The most important items from which we build our picture of the values placed on learning by the teacher are:

1. Collation and qualitative assessment of teacher's goal-setting and other value-laden statements
2. Frequency count of interactions with regard to classroom rules and routines, and children's behavior, which are compared with frequency counts directly related to curriculum content
3. Frequency counts of types of behavior praised and criticized, content of rewards and punishments, and differential allocation of praise and blame to different children
4. A series of further items, such as degree of interest seemingly shown in children's work, response to children's attempts at autonomous behavior in the curriculum area, teacher's allocation of time to various activities

Again these items are reinforced or contrasted with material from teacher interviews.

The teacher's structuring as reinforcing or undermining learning. Here we have a whole series of items which reveal whether classroom management is generally oriented toward learning, or toward orderliness and obedience more or less for their own sake; that is, whether and in what ways the classroom structuring encourages autonomy and positive-self feeling, along with cooperative—or benignly competitive—peer-group relations. Some of the above items involving frequency counts are reconsidered from this point of view, and are evaluated along with other items involving description or collation. Examples of these additional items are children's participation in planning, independence in getting supplies, handling of transitions, milk and cookies, and other routines. Again, parallel material from the teacher interview supplements or clarifies our judgment.

To recapitulate, we first try to define the model for learning which is being presented in a classroom, and then the extent to which motivation for learning, according to this model, is being imparted, (*a*) by the interest, meaning, and value the curriculum has for the children, (*b*) by the overt goals the teacher sets, and (*c*) by her reinforcement or undermining of learning goals through management of the classroom, her manner of rewarding and punishing the children, her style of relating to them, and her structuring of relations among them. Balancing each dimension or set of dimensions for the teacher, we have parallel items for the children: the extent to which (*a*) they show academic interest and initiative in their style of classroom participation, (*b*) see school learning as meaningful in terms of their own life expectations, (*c*) perceive and react to the teacher as a person who is *teaching,* rather than a person primarily to be feared and obeyed, manipulated and cajoled, or, as much as possible, ignored, and (*d*) see getting along with their peers as compatible with good school work.

In order to supplement classroom observation and child interview material, we have attempted to glean more of what is "getting across" to the children by seeking relations among the data collated on each individual child from the observations, the teacher interview, and the child interviews. We are seeking varying discernible trends in relations among the teacher's view of a child, her treatment of him in the classroom, the view other children have of him, and how he sees himself. We wish to know the basis for these variations, if any, and what their significance is to the transmission of motivation for learning.

Since the observations are focused on achieving as detailed an account as possible of every interaction between the teacher and the children, with each child identified by name, we can state not only whether the teacher is generally "supportive" or "undermining," but which children she supports, or undermines, and in what way, thus gaining greater insight into the values she is actually demonstrating in class. From her interview, we know which children she favors, and something of why (is it, for example, because they are good and quiet and always answer the way she wants, or because they are less docile, and therefore more interesting and challenging?). From the child interview, we see how the children define each other, and what characteristics they mention as a basis for liking, not liking, envying. We have material showing which children emerge most sharply as individuals in the classroom during the observation period, and the style of their emergence. Finally, there is some material on their level of performance (according to school-administered test scores) and on how they view themselves.

From an analysis of these data, we are attempting to see what alternatives are set up for the children in different classrooms, what are the different implications for the child who "goes along," who withdraws, or who rebels; for the child who is more concerned with pleasing authority, the child who is more concerned with work itself, the child who is more concerned with getting along with his peers, and so on. For instance, a child who is highly work-oriented meets a different response in a classroom where work orientation is really valued and built into the structure of classroom life than he would in a classroom where this is not so. Thus we are working with a concept of alternative choices and their corollary meanings, which vary from classroom to classroom, and tell the story of what is really "getting across" to children about how they should "get along."

Such an approach opens up several possibilities for analysis. First, it helps us define what constants there may be across schools according to the ethnic and class backgrounds of the children and to re-examine the hypothesis that the lower-class child allies himself with his peers against the "middle-class" teacher in a defensive attempt to maintain his self-respect, thus becoming less accessible to learning. Second, this approach helps us deal with the awkward fact that the same classroom has different effects on different children. The important point for analysis is that, although different children will act and react in different ways in a given classroom, they are all responding to the same situation, and, whether they accept them or not, they are all coping with the same meanings, values, and expectations, and dealing with them according to their own set of meanings and expectations.

In sum, after we view the model for learning which is being presented in a classroom, its meaning for the children, and the value that a teacher places on it through her handling of the children, we turn to assessing the degree to which a desire to learn is being reinforced or undermined by the classroom structuring. We are attempting to develop methods for dealing with this structuring as a composite of the teacher's action and implicit attitudes, and the meanings the children introduce as a result of their prior experience and future expectations.

BIBLIOGRAPHY

1. Ackerman, Walter I. "Teacher Competence and Pupil Change," *Harvard Educational Review,* Vol. 24 (1954), pp. 227–239.
2. Anderson, Harold H. "The Measurement of Domination and of Socially Integrative Behavior in Teachers' Contacts with Children," *Child Development,* Vol. 10, No. 2 (June 1939), pp. 73–89.
3. Anderson, Harold H., and Brewer, Helen M. *Studies of Teachers' Classroom Personalities, I: Dominative and Socially Integrative Behavior of Kindergarten Teachers.* Applied Psychology Monographs, 1945, No. 6.
4. Anderson, Harold H., and Brewer, Joseph E. *Studies of Teachers' Classroom Personalities, II: Effects of Teachers' Dominative and Integrative Contacts on Children's Classroom Behavior.* Applied Psychology Monographs, 1946, No. 8.
5. Anderson, Harold H., Brewer, Joseph E., and Reed, Mary Frances. *Studies of Teachers' Classroom Personalities, III: Follow-up Studies of the Effects of Dominative and Integrative Contacts on Children's Behavior.* Applied Psychology Monographs, 1946, No. 11.
6. Anderson, H. M. "A Study of Certain Criteria of Teacher Effectiveness, *Journal of Experimental Education,* Vol. 23 (1954), pp. 41–71.
7. Aschner, Mary J. McCue. "The Analysis of Classroom Discourse: A Method and Its Uses." Unpublished doctoral dissertation, University of Illinois, 1959. (On microfilm; Ann Arbor, Michigan.)
8. Aschner, Mary J. McCue. "The Language of Teaching," in B. Othanel Smith and Robert H. Ennis (Eds.), *Language and Concepts in Education.* Chicago: Rand McNally & Co., 1961. Pp. 112–126.
9. Aschner, Mary J., Gallagher, J. J., *et al.* "A System for Classifying Thought Processes in the Context of Classroom Verbal Interaction." Institute for Research on Exceptional Children, University of Illinois, 1962. (Mimeographed.)
9a. Bales, Robert F. *Interaction Process Analysis.* Cambridge, Mass.: Addison-Wesley, 1950.
10. Bales, R. F., and Strodtbeck, F. L. "Phases in Group Problem Solving,"

Journal of Abnormal and Social Psychology, Vol. 46 (October 1951), pp. 458–496.

11. Barr, A. S. *Characteristic Differences in the Teaching Performance of Good and Poor Teachers of the Social Studies.* Bloomington, Ill.: Public School Publishing Co., 1929.
12. Barr, A. S. "Measurement of Teacher Characteristics and Prediction of Teacher Efficiency," *Journal of Educational Research,* Vol. 22 (June 1952), p. 174.
13. Barr, A. S., Bechdolt, B. V., Coxe, W. W., Gage, N. L., Orleans, J. S., Remmers, H. H., and Ryans, D. G. "Report of the Committee on Criteria of Teacher Effectiveness," *Review of Educational Research,* Vol. 22 (1952), pp. 238–263.
14. Bellack, Arno A., and Huebner, Dwayne. "Teaching," *Review of Educational Research,* Vol. 30 (June 1960), pp. 246–257.
15. Blake, Robert. "A Frame of Reference for Behavorial Research," p. 5. (Multilithed.)
16. Brookover, W. B. "The Relation of Social Factors to Teaching Ability," *Journal of Experimental Education,* Vol. 13 (1945), pp. 191–205.
17. Bruner, Jerome S. *The Process of Education.* Cambridge, Mass.: Harvard University Press, 1961.
18. Cogan, M. L. "Theory and Design of a Study of Teacher-Pupil Interaction," *Harvard Educational Review,* Vol. 26, No. 4 (Fall 1956), pp. 315–342.
19. Cornell, F. G., Lindvall, C. M., and Saupe, J. L. *An Exploratory Measurement of Individualities of School and Classrooms.* Urbana, Ill.: College of Education, University of Illinois, Bureau of Educational Research, 1952.
20. Domas, S. J., and Tiedeman, D. V. "Teacher Competence: An Annotated Bibliography," *Journal of Experimental Education,* Vol. 19 (1950), pp. 101–218.
21. Flanders, Ned A. "Personal-Social Anxiety as a Factor in Experimental Learning Situations," *Journal of Educational Research,* Vol. 45 (October 1951), pp. 100–110.
22. Flanders, Ned A. "Teacher Influence in the Classroom." Paper presented at the first Teachers College Conference on Research and Theory in Teaching, April 13–14, 1962. (This volume, pp. 37–52.)
23. Flanders, Ned A. *Teacher Influence, Pupil Attitudes, and Achievement: Studies in Interaction Analysis.* U.S. Office of Education Cooperative Research Project, No. 397. Minneapolis: University of Minnesota, 1960. (Mimeographed.)
24. Gage, N. L. "The Handbook of Research on Teaching," *Journal of Teacher Education,* Vol. 13 (March 1962), p. 91.
25. Gage, N. L., *et al.* "Teachers' Understanding of Their Pupils and Pupils'

Ratings of Their Teachers." *Psychological Monograph: General and Applied,* Vol. 69, No. 21, Whole No. 406, 1956, p. 37.
26. Gallagher, J. J. *Analysis of Research on the Education of Gifted Children.* Springfield: State of Illinois, Office of the Superintendent of Public Instruction, 1960.
27. Gallagher, J. J., and Aschner, Mary J. McCue. "A Preliminary Report on Analyses of Classroom Interaction," *Merrill-Palmer Quarterly* (in press).
28. Getzels, J. W., and Jackson, P. W. *Creativity and Intelligence: Explorations with Gifted Students.* New York: John Wiley & Sons, Inc., 1962.
29. Getzels, Jacob W., and Thelen, Herbert A. "The Classroom Group as a Unique Social System," in *The Dynamics of Instructional Groups.* Chicago: University of Chicago Press, 1960. P. 56.
30. Gotham, R. E. "Personality and Teaching Efficiency," *Journal of Experimental Education,* Vol. 14 (1945), pp. 157–165.
31. Guilford, J. P., and Merrifield, P. R. *The Structure of Intellect Model: Its Uses and Implications.* Report No. 24; Reports from the Psychological Laboratory of the University of Southern California (April 1960).
32. Hellfritsch, A. G. "A Factor Analysis of Teacher Abilities," *Journal of Experimental Education,* Vol. 14 (1945), pp. 166–199.
33. Hughes, Marie M. "The Utah Study of the Assessment of Teaching." Paper presented at the first Teachers College Conference on Research and Theory in Teaching, April 13–14, 1962. (This volume, pp. 25–36.)
34. Hughes, Marie M., and Associates. *The Assessment of the Quality of Teaching: A Research Report.* U.S. Office of Education Cooperative Research Project, No. 353. Salt Lake City: University of Utah, 1959.
35. Jayne, C. D. "A Study of the Relationship Between Teaching Procedures and Educational Outcomes," *Journal of Experimental Education,* Vol. 14 (1945), pp. 101–134.
36a. Jones, R. D. "The Predicting of Teaching Efficiency from Objective Measures," *Journal of Experimental Education,* Vol. 15 (1946), pp. 85–99.
36. Kettner, N. W., Guilford, J. P., and Christensen, P. R. *A Factor-Analytic Study Across the Domains of Reasoning, Creativity, and Evaluation. Psychological Monograph* 73, No. 9; Whole No. 479, 1959.
37. LaDuke, C. V. "The Measurement of Teaching Ability: Study No. 3," *Journal of Experimental Education,* Vol. 14 (1945), pp. 75–100.
38. Lewin, Kurt. *Dynamic Theory of Personality.* New York: McGraw-Hill Book Co., 1935.
39. Lins, L. J. "The Prediction of Teaching Efficiency," *Journal of Experimental Education,* Vol. 15 (1946), pp. 2–60.
40. Lippitt, R., and White, R. K. "The 'Social Climate' of Children's Groups," in R. G. Barker, J. S. Kounin, and H. F. Wright (Eds.), *Child Behavior and Development.* New York: McGraw-Hill Book Co., 1943. Pp. 458–508.

41. Medley, D. M., and Mitzel, H. E. "Measuring Classroom Behavior by Systematic Observation," in N. L. Gage (Ed.), *Handbook of Research on Teaching*. Chicago: Rand McNally & Co., 1963.
42. Medley, D. M., and Mitzel, H. E. "Some Behavioral Correlates of Teacher Effectiveness," *Journal of Educational Psychology*, Vol. 50 (1959), pp. 239–246.
43. Medley, Donald M., and Mitzel, Harold E. "A Technique for Measuring Classroom Behavior," *Journal of Educational Psychology*, Vol. 49 (April 1958), pp. 86–92.
44. Mitzel, H. E., and Gross, Cecily. "The Development of Pupil Growth Criteria in Studies of Teacher Effectiveness," *Educational Research Bulletin*, Vol. 37 (1958), pp. 178–187 and 205–215.
45. Mitzel, Harold E., and Rabinowitz, William. "Assessing Social-Emotional Climate in the Classroom by Withall's Technique," *Psychological Monographs, General and Applied*, Vol. 67, No. 18, Whole No. 368 (1953), pp. 1–19.
46. Morsh, S. E., and Wilder, Eleanor W. "Identifying the Effective Instructor: A Review of the Quantitative Studies, 1900–1952," *USAF Personnel Training Research Center Research Bulletin* (1954), No. AFPTRC-TR-54-44.
47. Osgood, C. E., Suci, G. J., and Tannenbaum, P. H. *The Measurement of Meaning*. Urbana, Ill.: University of Illinois Press, 1957.
48. Perkins, H. V. "Climate Influences Group Learning," *Journal of Educational Research*, Vol. 45 (October 1951), pp. 115–119.
49. Rhode, A. R. "Explorations in Personality by the Sentence Completion Method," *Journal of Applied Psychology*, Vol. 30 (1946), pp. 169–181.
50. Sherif, M., and Wilson, M. O. (Eds.). *Group Relations at the Crossroad*. "An Analysis of Complaint Behavior," by Leon Festinger. New York: Harper & Brothers, 1953. Pp. 232–256.
51. Smith, D. E. P. "Fit Teaching Methods to Personality Structure," *High School Journal*, Vol. 39 (December 1955), pp. 167–171.
52. Scheuler, Herbert, Gold, Milton J., and Mitzel, Harold E. *The Use of Television for Improving Teacher Training and for Improving Measures of Student-Teaching Performance: Phase I. Improvement of Student Teaching*. Educational Media Branch of the U.S. Office of Education, Project No. 730035. New York: Hunter College of the City University of New York, 1962.
53. Smith, B. Othanel. "A Concept of Teaching," in B. Othanel Smith and Robert H. Ennis (Eds.), *Language and Concepts in Education*. Chicago: Rand McNally & Co., 1961. Pp. 86–101.
54. Smith, B. Othanel. "Toward a Theory of Teaching." Paper presented at the first Teachers College Conference on Research and Theory in Teaching, April 13–14, 1962. (This volume, pp. 1–10.)
55. Smith, B. Othanel, and Associates. *A Study of the Logic of Teaching:*

A Report on the First Phase of a Five-Year Research Project. U.S. Office of Education Cooperative Research Project, No. 258 (7257). Urbana, Ill.: University of Illinois, 1960.
56. Torrance, E. P. *Guiding Creative Talent.* Englewood Cliffs, N.J.: Prentice-Hall, Inc., 1962.
57. Wispe, Lauren G. "Evaluating Section Teaching Methods on the Introductory Course," *Journal of Educational Research,* Vol. 45, No. 3 (November 1951), pp. 161–186.
58. Withall, John. "The Development of a Technique for the Measurement of Social-Emotional Climate in Classrooms," *Journal of Experimental Education,* Vol. 17 (March 1949), pp. 347–361.
59. Withall, John. "Observing and Recording Behavior," *Review of Educational Research,* Vol. 30 (December 1960), pp. 496–512.
60. Wright, E., Wright, Muriel J., and Proctor, V. H. *Systematic Observation of Verbal Interaction as a Method of Comparing Mathematics Lessons.* U.S. Office of Education Cooperative Research Project, No. 816. St. Louis: Washington University, 1961.
61. Wrightstone, J. Wayne. *Appraisal of Newer Practices in Selected Public Schools.* New York: Bureau of Publications, Teachers College, Columbia University, 1935.